Paths of Resistance

The Writer's Craft
William Zinsser, Series Editor

EXTRAORDINARY LIVES
The Art and Craft of American Biography

INVENTING THE TRUTH
The Art and Craft of Memoir

SPIRITUAL QUESTS
The Art and Craft of Religious Writing

PATHS OF RESISTANCE
The Art and Craft of the Political Novel

Paths of Resistance

THE ART AND CRAFT
OF THE POLITICAL NOVEL

ISABEL ALLENDE / CHARLES McCARRY

MARGE PIERCY / ROBERT STONE

GORE VIDAL

Edited by WILLIAM ZINSSER

HOUGHTON MIFFLIN COMPANY

BOSTON

Introduction copyright © 1989 William K. Zinsser. "Writing As an Act of Hope," copyright © 1989 Isabel Allende. "A Strip of Exposed Film," copyright © 1989 Charles McCarry. "Active in Time and History," copyright © 1989 Marge Piercy. "We Are Not Excused," copyright © 1989 Robert Stone. "The Agreed-Upon Facts," copyright © 1989 Gore Vidal. For information about permission to reproduce selections from this book, write to Permissions, Houghton Mifflin Company, 2 Park Street, Boston, Massachusetts 02108.

Library of Congress Cataloging-in-Publication Data

Paths of resistance : the art and craft of the political novel / Isabel Allende . . . [et al.] ; edited by William Zinsser.
    p. cm. — (The Writer's craft)
    Bibliography: p.
    Contents: Introduction / William Zinsser — We are not excused / Robert Stone — Writing as an act of hope / Isabel Allende — A strip of exposed film / Charles McCarry — Active in time and history / Marge Piercy — The agreed-upon facts / Gore Vidal.
    ISBN 0-395-51426-6. — ISBN 0-395-51427-4 (pbk.)
    1. American fiction—20th century — History and criticism. 2. Political fiction, American — History and criticism. 3. Political fiction — Authorship.   I. Allende, Isabel. II. Zinsser, William Knowlton. III. Series.
PS374.P6P38 1989
813'.5409358 — dc20   89-32109
                     CIP

The poem "And Whose Creature Am I?" is reprinted from *My Mother's Body* by Marge Piercy. Copyright © 1985 by Marge Piercy. Reprinted by permission of Alfred A. Knopf, Inc.

Printed in the United States of America

D 10 9 8 7 6 5 4 3 2 1

Note

This book originated as a series of lectures — the fourth in an annual series of talks by writers on a particular aspect of the art and craft of writing, conceived and produced by Book-of-the-Month Club, Inc., and held at The New York Public Library. The Club would like to thank Vartan Gregorian, former president of the Library, and David Cronin, coordinator of public education programs, for the Library's gracious collaboration as host of the series.

Three of the talks are followed by brief excerpts from the question-and-answer period that made further points about the writing process.

Contents

WILLIAM ZINSSER

Introduction

THIS BOOK originated as a series of talks on the art and craft of the political novel. The series was conceived by the Book-of-the-Month Club, co-sponsored by The New York Public Library, and held at the Library on successive Thursday evenings in the winter of 1988. It was the fourth season for the lectures. In three earlier series, which also became books, writers talked about the art and craft of biography (*Extraordinary Lives*), memoir (*Inventing the Truth*) and religious writing (*Spiritual Quests*). The writers were asked to be personal and specific — to explain how they went about their work.

In this fourth series something different happened: the "how" changed to "why." "Political," obviously, was no ordinary adjective; it turned out to be a word with no end of reverberations, many of them new within the adult life of the five writers — the result of stirrings of conscience and resistance both at home and abroad, often in remote corners of Asia, Africa and Latin America. For these writers, "political" was nothing less than their agenda, their reason for writing, their why.

Robert Stone, for instance, when he began writing novels, knew what his subject would be. His subject was America. Yet the two novels that elevated him to the first rank of American authors had their origin in places far from home. *Dog Soldiers*, which won the National Book Award in 1974, was initially set in Saigon; it was a story of America in Vietnam. Gradually, however, narrative logic told Stone that his real subject was the reverse — the story of Vietnam in America, of the miasma that was choking the United States because of its war ten thousand miles away — just as his next novel, *A Flag for Sunrise*, though set in Central America, was really the story of America's corrosive "overlordship" (as he once called it) in Nicaragua. Politically, the roots of both novels went back to Washington.

For Isabel Allende, the niece of Chile's assassinated president Salvador Allende, the politics of her homeland was inseparable from her existence as a woman and as a writer. "The military coup in Chile changed everything," she once recalled, "and I felt that my life had been cut into pieces." That rupture would become one of the main threads in her eloquent novel *The House of the Spirits*, a three-generation tapestry about a patrician family not unlike her own in a country not unlike Chile, just as her subsequent novel, *Of Love and Shadows*, was based on the discovery of fifteen bodies — victims of political persecution — in an abandoned Chilean mine. In Latin America, Isabel Allende says, politics is a constant presence.

Charles McCarry has written six "novels of political intelligence" — most recently *The Bride of the Wilderness* — that he thinks of as one novel. All of them are chronicles of an American family named Christopher whose members have been involved in the world of politics and secret intelligence since 1700. Broadly, he once explained, they are about "love, death, betrayal and the American dream"; specifically, they are about "the invisible government." In his own career McCarry has worked for the government in positions of varying visibility, and his best-known nonfiction book, *Citizen Nader*, written before he launched the Christophers on three centuries of espionage, is about the political outsider Ralph Nader.

McCarry is the only one of these authors who actually lives in Washington.

Marge Piercy is a poet, a novelist and a feminist. "Because I'm a feminist, the personal is political and the political is personal," she once explained. This credo is at the heart of her eight novels — notably, *Woman on the Edge of Time*, which is about a feminist Utopian society; *Vida*, the story of a woman political fugitive in the sixties antiwar movement; and *Gone to Soldiers*, a novel about how World War II changed the social attitudes of Americans — as well as her many volumes of poetry, in which she has dealt with "everything from the politics of aging and weight to the importance of seeing oneself as part of nature rather than apart from nature." One of her main targets is the notion that politics is somehow separate from art. "Social values," she says, "are always built into structures that use words."

Gore Vidal needs no introduction as a political animal. His spacious political novels about the shaping figures and currents of American constitutional life — *Burr, Lincoln, 1876, Empire* and *Washington, D.C.* — have basked not only in huge popularity but in critical acclaim. Politics has also been a major preoccupation in his plays, such as *The Best Man*, in his four books of essays (for example, *An Evening with Richard*

Introduction

Nixon and *The Second American Revolution,* which won the National Book Critics Circle Award for criticism in 1982), and in his life; he grew up in Washington, the grandson of Senator Thomas Gore, and has twice run for congressional office himself, once in California and once in New York. A writer of refreshing candor, Vidal has never quailed from saying what he thinks. He also disproves the theory — as did the politician who most interests him, Abraham Lincoln — that wit and politics don't mix. Humor in his writing is a solvent for ideas that go against the grain.

This was the baggage that the five writers brought to their talks at The New York Public Library. Established authority was their common subject — how it is exercised, resisted or eroded — and one of their common themes was the fact that their craft would always be the prisoner of attitudes and events at the moment of their books' publication.

"Even if you're not writing for political reasons," Charles McCarry says, "the political climate at a given time has a great deal to do with what you can get away with. The Horatio Alger books, which are political novels in a very pure and simple form, wouldn't have made the same splash in any time but their own, and André Malraux's *Man's Fate,* probably the most

admired political novel of the first half of the twentieth century, was also published at exactly the right
moment, in 1933. Nobody like Alger's noble urchins
or Malraux's noble assassin ever existed on this planet
except in the mind of an idealist.

"And that of course is the difficulty. It's possible,
if you have a political point of view, to see all writing
in political terms," McCarry says, noting that in the
Book of Exodus God was "clearly talking politics."
So harsh is the difficulty that a successful marriage of
politics and literature is seldom brought off, and only
a writer great enough to exalt the form can do it.
McCarry's case in point is Mark Twain. "The relationship between Huckleberry Finn and Jim is an
examination of the most profound political question
in the history of the United States: slavery. But *The
Adventures of Huckleberry Finn* clearly provides all
the evidence needed that a political novel can be a
work of art."

How to manage this balancing act is a major
concern of these five writers. "Any novel of serious
intent argues for the significance of its story," says
Robert Stone. Significance, however, is a dreary actor,
best kept hidden in the wings. "I think the key is to
establish a connection between political forces and
individual lives," Stone says, recalling the birth of the

book that was to become *A Flag for Sunrise*. "The longer I stayed in Nicaragua, the more I began to hear stories. After a while the stories began to form a pattern that conformed to a sense I had of the history of Central America. This band of republics between the Andes and the Grijalva River seemed to be placed by their gods in a very fateful situation. They seemed to have drawn the most violent conquistadors and the most fanatical inquisitors. The arriving Spaniards had found holy wells of human sacrifice. There, racial and social oppression had always been at its most severe. The fertile soil of the place seemed to bring forth things to provoke the appetite rather than things to nourish — plantation crops for your sweet tooth or for your head. They were all labor-intensive, high-profit items: bananas, of course, and coffee, chocolate, tobacco, chicle, emeralds, marijuana, cocaine. And since my subject was America, and the United States had been involved there for so long, I decided to put down the book I was writing and to begin a new one." Storytelling, Stone reminds us, is not a luxury; it's a staple that we "urgently require — almost as necessary as bread. We can't imagine ourselves without it."

For Isabel Allende, stories are her only hope of harnessing "a land of crazy, illuminated people." Western critics often ask, she says, how Latin American authors "dare to invent those incredible lies of young women who fly to heaven wrapped in linen sheets; of black emperors who build fortresses with cement and the blood of emasculated bulls; of outlaws who die of hunger in the Amazon with bags full of emeralds on their backs; of ancient tyrants who order their mothers to be flogged naked in front of the troops and modern tyrants who order children to be tortured in front of their parents; of revolutions made with machetes, bullets, poems and kisses." These, she insists, are not pathological ravings. "They are written in our history; we can find them every day in our newspapers; we hear them in the streets; we suffer them frequently in our own lives." Violence is the dark stain in Allende's talk, coloring all experience; Latin Americans exist, she says, on the borderline of violence. "Maybe the most important reason for writing is to prevent the erosion of time, so that memories will not be blown away by the wind. In a novel we can give an illusory order to chaos."

It is through the telling of stories that the political novelist discovers what they add up to. "I assemble what is known, then start to look for a pattern," says Gore Vidal. "In the process of writing the anecdotes of the past I found that life became more comprehensible and the world more tolerable," says Isabel Allende. "We want to see all this mess mean something, even if what we discover is a shape perhaps beautiful but not necessarily comforting," says Marge Piercy. "In the novel, as in politics and in life itself," says Charles McCarry, "you cannot know what the consequences of any act will be until you come to the end." The ultimate consequence, of course — gruesome beyond the imagining of any author at the time of these talks, in the pre-Rushdie era — is a sentence of death for the act of writing.

Alone among these five novelists, Gore Vidal is telling stories about people who actually lived and is therefore accountable to historical truth. But even he has discovered that truth is a variable commodity, shifting with the political tides of the day, regardless of what happened yesterday. "Although I try to make the agreed-upon facts as accurate as possible," he says, "I always use the phrase 'agreed-upon' because what we know of a figure as recent as, let's say, Theodore Roosevelt is not only not the whole truth — an impossibility anyway — but the so-called facts are often contradicted by other facts. So one must select, and it is in selection that literature begins. To begin with, *whose* facts do you agree with?"

On this question Vidal, as usual, does not find himself aligned with Academia — specifically, with the "scholar-squirrels" who believe that "there is a final Truth, revealed only to the tenured." His novels run afoul of the tendency of each generation of scholars to rearrange the agreed-upon facts about "the illustrious dead" to fit the political needs of the times. He cites one critic's rousing attack on his *Lincoln* which stated that "there is no convincing evidence" for Vidal's claim that as late as April 1865, Lincoln was still planning to colonize freed slaves outside the United States.

"This is a delicate point in the 1980s, when no national saint can be suspected of racism," Vidal says, noting that Lincoln did in fact continue until his death to entertain the idea of removing to another country the freed Negro population. "What is going on here is a deliberate revision," not only of Lincoln but of the critic's own earlier writing, "to serve the saint in the 1980s, as opposed to the saint at earlier times, when blacks were still colored, having only just stopped being Negroes. In colored and Negro days the saint would have wanted them out of the country, as Lincoln did. But in the age of Martin Luther King, Jr., even the most covertly racist of school boards must agree that a saint like Abraham Lincoln could never have wanted a single black person to leave freedom's land, much less bravery's home.

"So all the hagiographers are redoing their plaster images," Vidal says, and anyone who dares to draw attention to the discrepancy is "a very bad person indeed." Vidal has never minded being a very bad person in the eyes of hagiographers or, for that matter, anyone else. On the contrary, he accepts it as a condition of his trade and just another example of politics at work, sanitizing yesterday's reality. "It is my radical view," Vidal says, "that Americans are now sufficiently mature to be shown Lincoln as close to the original as possible."

Marge Piercy feels equally out in the cold. She finds American critics and academics scornful of politically conscious work, especially the work of feminist and leftist writers, which they consider cruder and more naïve than "work that simply embodies currently held notions." They prefer work that doesn't trouble the waters — novels, that is, which mirror the writer's own snug world and ask no hard questions. "One reason why many American novelists have atrophied, producing their best work out of the concerns of late adolescence and early childhood," Piercy says, "is that since they don't care to grapple with or even identify the moving forces in their society, they can't understand more than a few stories. If we view the world as static, we lack perspective on the lives we are creating. We must be able to feel ourselves active in time and history."

What emerges from her talk is a portrait of the political novelist as a chronic outsider, saying things that reviewers don't want to hear, writing about people they don't want to meet. "Reviewers don't perceive books as having a political dimension when the ideas are congruent with the reviewers' own attitudes or with those they're used to hearing discussed at parties. But when reviewers read novels whose attitudes offend them or clash with their own ideas, they perceive those novels as political and polemical, and they attack them. They strongly resist fiction that takes a collective stance, that sees each character as embedded in history and in an economic and social web."

Summing up what keeps her going as a political novelist, Marge Piercy says, "I'm responsible to people with buried lives."

The novelist E. L. Doctorow once said that what writers do is to "distribute the suffering so that it can be borne." No less vividly, Isabel Allende says that what today's political novelists do is to "give both men and women a chance to become better people and to share the heavy burden of this planet. This is the true political literature of our time." At its strongest this literature is being written today, she says, "by those who stand unsheltered by the system: blacks, Indians, homosexuals, exiles and, especially, women — the crazy people of the world, who dare to believe in their own force. We write as an act of human solidarity and commitment to the future. We want to change the rules, even if we won't live long enough to see the results."

This is perilous terrain — idealism is the enemy of art, and even optimism is risky. As Charles McCarry reminds us, the political novelist is in constant danger of writing what he believes instead of what he knows. He recalls his first exposure, as a boy, to "the very model of a political novel" — a potboiler by Zane Grey which he says, could be published today as a story of Afghanistan or Israel or Nicaragua just by changing the details. But it still wouldn't be a novel; it would be propaganda. "The propagandist sees things as he thinks they should be; the novelist must see things as they are," says McCarry. "Don't ask real novelists to write wish-fulfillment fantasies," says Marge Piercy. "Above all, you must not sentimentalize," says Robert Stone. All three are steeling themselves against the very instincts that impel them to write political novels in the first place. What they are saying is: If you want to change the world, don't try to change the world. Write the truth, and write clearly.

Yet within the disciplined artist there's no hiding the idealist. "I feel that writing is an act of hope," says Isabel Allende. She is willing to run the literary risk of being a simple messenger of hope to a continent that has almost none. "A book is not an end in itself; it is only a way to touch someone. The writer of good will carries a lamp to illuminate the dark corners."

Robert Stone is no less driven by the strength of his character to be a carrier of lamps, and perhaps he speaks for all political literature when he says, "Moments occur when we amaze each other with acts of hope, acts of courage that can make one proud to be human. The fact is that we absolutely require the elevated image of ourselves that we indulge." Lacking such an image, "we would never be capable of the extensions of ourselves that are required of us."

ROBERT STONE

We Are Not Excused

I'D LIKE TO approach the subject of the political novel somewhat obliquely. Last spring the writer and critic William Gass wrote an article in *Harper's Magazine* called "Goodness Knows Nothing of Beauty," which toyed with the proposition that art and moral aspiration were mutually distant. Statements of this view often seek to replicate in their style the kind of cool, amoral elegance that they claim for good art, and Mr. Gass's piece is not in this regard exceptional. It is characterized by paradox, alliteration and a faintly decadent naughtiness suggestive of intense sophistication.

In the end, as such pieces often do, it resolves itself solipsistically — that is, it explains itself away in terms of its own moral and aesthetic definitions. But it's interesting to see this old opposition between art and morality appear again, offered by a commentator usually so wise and insightful. "To be a preacher is to bring your sense of sin to the front of the church," says Mr. Gass, "but to be an artist is to give to every mean and ardent, petty and profound feature of the soul a glorious godlike shape."

If this means that you get no points in art for good intentions, no one would argue. But I find here echoes of an old romantic antinomian tendency that goes back at least to Nietzsche. It has been argued by people as different as Ortega y Gasset and Oscar Wilde; by Joyce, speaking in character as Stephen Dedalus; and by Shaw during the period when he was writing *Major Barbara* and, it now appears, attempting to invent fascism.

In this antinomian vision, morality and art are independent and even in opposition. On the right squats morality. It may be imagined as a neo-Gothic structure, immense, ornate and sterile. Its self-satisfaction, lack of imagination and philistine sentimentality are advertised in its every plane and line. Architecturally, it resembles the Mormon Tabernacle, the one in downtown Salt Lake City, not the Hollywood-Biblical one on Santa Monica Boulevard. And on the left — art. Art is nothing but beautiful. Art is like a black panther. It has the glamour of the desperado. Art is radical, the appealing cousin of crime. Never a dull moment with art. Morality, in this view, is not only its opposite but its enemy.

This claim of estrangement between morality and art retains its currency for an excellent reason: it's fun. It's agreeable for an artist to imagine himself as a Zarathustran rope dancer, balanced against eternity up in the ozone and thin light, while far below the eunuchs of the brown temple of morality whine platitudes at each other in the incense-ridden noonday darkness. "Look before you leap." "A stitch in time saves nine."

But let us pursue the notion. Let us imagine the novel, for example, freed completely from moral considerations. What would that be like? One thing it might be like is one of the antinovels that M. Robbe-Grillet gave us during the fifties and sixties. These are novels without any moral context, but they are similarly without characters, plots, beginnings or endings. Surely such an exercise in doing without something serves to reinforce the idea of its necessity. Is it possible to postulate the idea of a successful novel about people, or about animals, for that matter, in which the living of life is reflected, that exists beyond the signal area of any moral reference points?

What about the comic novel? Let's eliminate at the outset the obviously sentimental or political comedies that have a message at their core. Let's take the work of two writers who have written very funny books and who aren't usually thought of as kindly humanistic sages: William Burroughs and Evelyn Waugh.

Naked Lunch is the prototypical Burroughs novel, and like all the others, it's full of cruelty — not just sadism but cruelty. The element of sci-fi political satire that it contains is sometimes claimed as representing a moral dimension, though I think that's really bogus. The moral element in the work of William Burroughs is in its very humor. In the grimmest imaginable places — in the grammar of drug addiction, in the violence and treachery of the addict's world — Burroughs finds laughter. The laughter itself is a primary moral response. Laughter represents a rebellion against chaos, a rejection of evil and an affirmation of balance and soundness.

Let me give an example. I was once given a description of the meanest bar in the world. It was not far from here, and it catered to the evil. To be at home in this place you had to be self-consciously corrupt and completely without mercy. You had to be utterly depraved. In this place, the way it was told to me, there were two rules. The first was "no rugby shirts" and the second was "no laughing." We must assume that the people who run places like that know what they're doing.

Now Evelyn Waugh seems to have been lacking in all the qualities that we philanthropists find congenial. A bully, a coward, a Fascist, a despiser of minorities and the poor, a groveler before the rich and powerful, Waugh was surely one of the worst human beings ever to become a major novelist. But paradoxically, his life and work provide us with a ringing confirmation of the dependence of serious fiction on morality. By borrowing — spuriously or otherwise, it doesn't matter — the certainties of Catholicism, Waugh was able to infuse his best work with the moral center that makes it great. The worldly lives described in the *Men at Arms* trilogy and in *Brideshead Revisited* are constantly being measured against a rigorous neo-Jansenist Christianity. In these books the invisible world becomes the real one, and its meanings constitute the truth that underlies the confusion of desires in which the characters struggle.

William Gass's essay starts by having us ask ourselves whether we would rescue an infant or a Botticelli painting if we saw both of them being washed out to sea and could only salvage one. The Botticelli is a masterpiece, the baby is only a potential human being. After prescribing us this brisk, antinomian exercise, Gass commences to deflate his own balloon by running it on the thorns of common sense. He refers to the historical struggle against censorship, as though this somehow established art's essentially unmoral character, and then admits that each censoring hierarchy was reacting to whatever inadequacies of its moral system were being challenged by the work in question. He reminds us that good books were written by bad people, and he ends with the truism that propaganda can't justify bad art or bad writing, which hardly earns the Faustian bombast of the title "Goodness Knows Nothing of Beauty."

There are few statements in the essay that Gass doesn't obviate or contradict in his next paragraph. But there is one that stays unforsworn and unqualified. He refers to Keats's identification of beauty with truth and vice versa as a fatuous little motto. This is being unkind to a perfectly nice axiom, and perhaps it's a hasty judgment. Surely we should meditate for a moment on this most appealing sentiment. Is it true?

Concerning life, it's a question that we cannot finally answer. I think it tends to be true. The explanation at the core of one of nature's mysteries is often edifying. Job cuts through to the substance of it when he questions the beneficence of God. In the end he learns that God is worshipful, that God's majesty and holiness suffuse the universe. This is what the medieval mystic Julian of Norwich was referring to when she wrote, "All shall be well and all shall be well and all manner of things shall be well." In terms of Western tradition it should be true that truth is beauty. Even if you take God out of it, the grimmest principles of existence have their symmetry. All the same, there can be a hundred different explanations for things, and every one of them beautiful and none of them true.

But in art, isn't it always true? Surely every aesthetic response entails a recognition. What standard do we hold up to art other than things themselves? And what do we require from art if not a reflection of things, of our lives, in all their variety?

To narrow the focus now, I'd like to talk about the practical art form that I know most about: the novel. We in the Western world are what the Moslems call "people of the book." Our prototypical book in this culture is the Bible, and that's true whether or not we are believers or whether we were brought up by believers. After centuries of being Christians and Jews our context and our perceptions continue to be conditioned by the Bible's narratives. Even today in our contemporary secularized world, if I talk about "the good book" you will realize which volume I'm referring to.

It's hard to overestimate the impact of the Bible on our civilization and our language. The novel came into existence with the rise of a literate mass readership, and the greatest vehicle of mass literacy in the English-speaking world was the King James Bible. It was the great primer.

The Bible is unique among religious books in the relationship it defines between God and man and in the view it takes of human life. The narratives about people in the books of the Bible are thought to mean something. They are thought to be significant. This implies that the corporeal world in which people live is not an illusion to be overcome, or a shadowland reflecting the void, but an instrument of God's will. What people do on earth matters, because earth is really the only place where things are happening. So for centuries we have been reflecting on peculiar things, like why Adam ate the fruit and how Abraham could have been ready to sacrifice his son, and asking ourselves: What does this mean? What are these people trying to tell me with this strange story?

What can I learn from it? How does it bear on my situation?

It follows from the attitude reflected in the Bible that human life is meaningful. Human annals become charged. They become an entity, history. History then becomes more than just a story; it becomes a process, the unfolding of a design, something with a dynamic that can be uncovered.

Any novel of serious intent argues for the significance of its story. A reader holds the characters in judgment, investing sympathy or withholding it and always alert for recognitions, hoping to see his lonely state reflected in someone else's story, however exotic or remote its setting may be. So it's impossible for fiction to be other than a moral enterprise.

There are two basic facts in life. We are out here in this stuff, whatever it is, whatever it's called . . . Thursday. And we are not alone out here. Fortunately, we have each other. Unfortunately, we have each other. At which point, politics necessarily commences.

There is no brown temple where morality resides. There is no high wire above it where the artist whirls in freedom. If there's a wire, it's the wire we're all on out here, the one we live on. I think we imagine, we contemporary people, that somewhere readily at hand is a vast body of truth and wisdom, there to be called upon when the necessity arises. We imagine that beneath our feet is a vast, complex structure called civilization that will support our caperings. But of course that's not how life is.

Most journalists who worked in Vietnam during the war were oppressed by the extreme difficulty of translating what they saw into words. It wasn't necessarily that it was so uniquely horrible; it was that the brutality and confusion one experienced seemed to lose something when rendered into language. Somehow, in describing the situation so that it could be set up in columns of type, one always seemed to be cleaning it up. As I pondered this process a moment of illumination struck me: we are forever cleaning up our act. Not only in describing ourselves but in imagining ourselves we project a self-image that is considerably idealized. In our relationships with other people we conventionalize ourselves so as not to frighten them with our primary process. And just as we individually cultivate an elevated image of ourselves, so we collectively conspire as nations, as peoples, as humankind, to create a fictional exemplar of our collective selves, our selves as we have agreed to imagine ourselves.

But this is not the whole story. Though we are only what we are, we have this amazing ability to extend, to transcend the grimmest circumstances. Moments occur when we amaze each other with acts of hope, acts of courage that can make one proud to be human. The fact is that we absolutely require the elevated image of ourselves that we indulge. If we didn't idealize ourselves, if we accepted only the reality of ourselves as we are most of the time, we would never be capable of the extensions of ourselves that are required of us.

Things are in the saddle, Emerson said, and ride mankind. Whirl is king. Things happen ruthlessly, without mercy; the elemental force of things bears down on us. From one moment to the next we hardly know what's going on, let alone what it all means. Civilization is not structure. It's a notion — sometimes a very distant notion. It can be blown away in a second. In the worst of times there is little of it around.

What is civilization, then? What is morality? There are fictions that sometimes seem to come almost from another place. They are stories, but stories that we urgently require. It's much harder to act well than we are ready to admit. It can be extremely hard to act fairly sensibly, let alone well.

Storytelling is not a luxury to humanity; it's almost as necessary as bread. We can't imagine ourselves without it. The self is a story: our individual, brief place in history is compounded of stories — stories that we shape inwardly and outwardly to make them more agreeable and hence more useful. As dreams are to waking life, so fiction is to reality. The brain can't function without clearing its circuits during sleep, nor can we contemplate and analyze our situation without living some of the time in the world of imagination, that doorway to the interior self.

Having talked about the uses of fiction, I'd like to be more specifically political. Writers, it seems to me, discharge their social responsibility by writing as well — or, to employ a Hemingwayesque locution, as well and truly — as they can. The writer who betrays his calling is the one who, for commercial or political reasons, vulgarizes his own perception and imagination and his rendering of them. Meretricious writing tries to conventionalize what it describes in order to make it safer and easier to take. It may do this to conform to a political agenda that is seen as somehow overriding mere literary considerations or, under commercial pressures, to appeal to what are seen as the limitations of a mass audience. The effect of such conventionalized, vulgarized writing is pernicious. The practice of fiction is an act against loneliness, an appeal to community, a bet on the possibility that the enormous gulf that separates one human being from another can be bridged. It has a responsibility to understand and to illustrate the varieties of the human condition in order that consciousness may be enlarged.

Meretricious fiction does the opposite of what fiction is supposed to do. The reassurance that it offers is superficial: in the end it makes life appear circumscribed. It makes reality appear limited and bound by convention, and as a result it increases each person's loneliness and isolation. When the content of fiction is limited to one definition of acceptability, people are abandoned to the beating of their own hearts, to imagine that things which wound them, drive them and inspire them may be a kind of aberration particular to themselves.

Now let me talk a little about my own work. A political situation is an ideal subject for a novel. A revolution, a war, any upheaval liberates some people from the prison of the self as it invites others to play out their personal dramas on a larger stage. One sees people caught up in things that transcend the personal, but always bringing their own needs and desires to bear. People make pleasant and unpleasant discoveries about each other and themselves. The elements of drama descend on ordinary people and ordinary lives.

In my work the subject has always been America in one aspect or another. I wrote my first book, *A Hall of Mirrors*, after spending a year in the Deep South that happened to coincide with the first sit-ins and the beginning of the struggle against segregation — and also with the reaction to it. It was written during a period of great change in this country, the first half of the 1960s. It centered on the exploitation of the electronic media by the extreme right, a phenomenon that we haven't altogether put behind us.

I put everything I knew and everything I felt into *A Hall of Mirrors*. I mean, every single thing I knew went into it, and I gave my characters names with the maximum number of letters because I thought that would make them more substantial. All my quarrels with America went into it. I had been in New Orleans with my girlfriend for a year and we had been very poor. Mine was definitely a street-level encounter with the city, and I think that enriched the book — and also gave it some political drive. After that I was at loose ends until I got myself hired to go to Vietnam.

In Vietnam I found a mistake ten thousand miles long, a mistake on the American scale. And since America was my subject, I began to write a novel set in Saigon. As it progressed I realized that the logic of the thing required that everybody make their way back home to the America of the early seventies. That, I think, was a particularly evil period in this country. The cities were ruined, crime was rampant, all the due bills extended from the sixties had come up for presentation.

Then, like a bad penny, in the mid-seventies I showed up in Central America. I hadn't gone there to write a political novel. When I went for the first time, in 1976, things seemed quiet. Nobody in this country knew where Huehuetenango was, or Managua. Nicaragua was in an old Andrews Sisters lyric.

I went to the island of Roatán, on the coast of Honduras, to go diving. I was at work on a different book, which is still unfinished. In Honduras I met a man and two women who were driving down to Managua. They asked me if I wanted a ride, so I went. I stayed with them in Managua for a while, and one day I found myself at a cocktail party in the presidential palace. It's a small place and it was social. Anastasio Somoza and his family had been running Nicaragua for a long time, and they seemed secure enough in their power — at least to me. The presidential palace was in the middle of a fallen city. From a distance, downtown Managua looked like a park, it was so green. When one got a closer look one could see that the green was that of vegetation growing over the rubble where the center of the city had collapsed on Christmas Eve, 1972. The presidential palace stood unscathed in the middle of the destruction. Around it was a kind of free-fire zone of scrub jungle where no one was permitted to enter. The palace stood just beyond the effective mortar range from the nearest habitation.

As I said, I was working on another book, and this was supposed to be a vacation. But the longer I stayed in Nicaragua, the more I began to hear stories. After a while the stories began to form a pattern that conformed to a sense I had of the history of Central America. This band of republics between the Andes and the Grijalva River seemed to be placed by their gods in a very fateful situation. They seemed to have drawn the most violent conquistadors and the most fanatical inquisitors. The arriving Spaniards had found holy wells of human sacrifice. There, racial and social oppression had always been severe. The fertile soil of the place seemed to bring forth things to provoke the appetite rather than things to nourish — rare baubles and rich toys, plantation crops for your sweet tooth or for your head. They were all labor-intensive, high-profit items: bananas, of course, and coffee, chocolate, tobacco, chicle, emeralds, marijuana, cocaine. And since my subject was America, and the United States had been involved there for so long, by the time I got back to the States I had decided to put down the book I was writing and to begin a new one, and the new one became my third novel, my third political novel, *A Flag for Sunrise*.

The political novel is a very various thing — the category includes so many different kinds of books. *The Charterhouse of Parma*, *Nostromo*, *Barnaby Rudge*, *A Tale of Two Cities* and *All the King's Men* are all political novels, all very different in spirit. I think a successful political novel requires a knowledge — legitimately or illegitimately acquired, intuitive or empirical — of the situation that one chooses to write about. Political commitment is not required, although eventually most authors maneuver themselves into a stand. I think the key is to establish the connection between political forces and individual lives. The questions to address are: How do social and political forces condition individual lives? How do the personal qualities of the players condition their political direction?

You have to cast the net of your sympathies fairly wide. You should be able to imagine your way into the personas of many different people with different ways of thinking and believing. The aspiring political novelist might spend a little time every morning meditating on the interior life of General Noriega, a man who actually exists. As far as political satire goes, you should remember that the best satire requires a certain subversive sympathy for your subject.

Above all, you must not sentimentalize. Sentimentality is the great enemy of genuine sentiment. Commitment can be useful because it brings a degree of passion to bear. But it's also dangerous. Nothing is free in the world. To be a contented partisan of one side or another you have to sell something. In exchange for your contentment you have to give up a measure of critical judgment. Because so much of serious politics in this century consists of violence, this can be a morally enervating exercise. Moral enervation is bad for writers.

I've always disliked statements that wind up with a kind of sappy harmony by saying that, well, everything is like everything else. But I'm afraid I must inflict something like that on you. Anything I've said this evening can be applied with very little adjustment to the novel in general. The political novel is not really a genre; its history is far too various. In terms of my own work, its element is what I believe to be the transitory nature of moral perception. I think it's extremely difficult for people to identify and act upon the right. The world is full of illusion. We carry nemesis inside us — almost, it seems, by design. But we are not excused.

Back in the sixties when we were all crazy, a friend of mine composed a little ditty that sums up the two-steps-forward, one-step-back nature of humanity's march: "Of offering more than what we can deliver, we have a bad habit, it is true. But we have to offer more than what we can deliver to be able to deliver what we do."

———

Q. What do you like about writing? Do you like being heard?

A. What I like about it is how much sense you can make of things. I think the most difficult thing we have to contend with is the confusion of things, the multiplicity of things. It's very satisfying to be able to quietly set down what you think is going on. It's good for your head. And I like that.

Q. What do you learn as a writer?

A. You learn things about yourself. You learn what you think. The wonderful thing about writing is that you're constantly having to ask yourself questions. It makes you function morally. It makes you function intellectually. That's the great pleasure and great reward of writing.

ISABEL ALLENDE

Writing As an Act of Hope

IN EVERY INTERVIEW during the last few years I encountered two questions that forced me to define myself as a writer and as a human being: Why do I write? And who do I write for? Tonight I will try to answer those questions.

In 1981, in Caracas, I put a sheet of paper in my typewriter and wrote the first sentence of *The House of the Spirits:* "Barabbas came to us by sea." At that moment I didn't know why I was doing it, or for whom. In fact, I assumed that no one would ever read it except my mother, who reads everything I write. I was not even conscious that I was writing a novel. I thought I was writing a letter — a spiritual letter to my grandfather, a formidable old patriarch, whom

I loved dearly. He had reached almost one hundred years of age and decided that he was too tired to go on living, so he sat in his armchair and refused to drink or eat, calling for Death, who was kind enough to take him very soon.

I wanted to bid him farewell, but I couldn't go back to Chile, and I knew that calling him on the telephone was useless, so I began this letter. I wanted to tell him that he could go in peace because all his memories were with me. I had forgotten nothing. I had all his anecdotes, all the characters of the family, and to prove it I began writing the story of Rose, the fiancée my grandfather had had, who is called Rose the Beautiful in the book. She really existed; she's not a copy from García Márquez, as some people have said.

For a year I wrote every night with no hesitation or plan. Words came out like a violent torrent. I had thousands of untold words stuck in my chest, threatening to choke me. The long silence of exile was turning me to stone; I needed to open a valve and let the river of secret words find a way out. At the end of that year there were five hundred pages on my table; it didn't look like a letter anymore. On the other hand, my grandfather had died long before, so the spiritual message had already reached him. So I thought, "Well, maybe in this way I can tell some other people about him, and about my country, and about my family and myself." So I just organized it a little bit, tied the manuscript with a pink ribbon for luck, and took it to some publishers.

The spirit of my grandmother was protecting the book from the very beginning, so it was refused everywhere in Venezuela. Nobody wanted it — it was too long; I was a woman; nobody knew me. So I sent it by mail to Spain, and the book was published there. It had reviews, and it was translated and distributed in other countries.

In the process of writing the anecdotes of the past, and recalling the emotions and pains of my fate, and telling part of the history of my country, I found that life became more comprehensible and the world more tolerable. I felt that my roots had been recovered and that during that patient exercise of daily writing I had also recovered my own soul. I felt at that time that writing was unavoidable — that I couldn't keep away from it. Writing is such a pleasure; it is always a private orgy, creating and recreating the world according to my own laws, fulfilling in those pages all my dreams and exorcising some of my demons.

But that is a rather simple explanation. There are other reasons for writing.

Six years and three books have passed since *The*

House of the Spirits. Many things have changed for me in that time. I can no longer pretend to be naïve, or elude questions, or find refuge in irony. Now I am constantly confronted by my readers, and they can be very tough. It's not enough to write in a state of trance, overwhelmed by the desire to tell a story. One has to be responsible for each word, each idea. Be very careful: the written word cannot be erased.

I began to receive academic papers from American universities about the symbols in my books, or the metaphors, or the colors, or the names. I'm always very scared by them. I just received three different papers on Barabbas, the dog. One of them says that he symbolizes the innocence of Clara because he accompanies her during her youth, and when she falls in love, symbolically, the dog dies in a pool of blood. That means the sexual act, it seems. The second paper says that the dog represents repression — the militarists — and the third paper says that he is the male part of Clara, the hidden, dark, big beast in her. Well, really, Barabbas was just the dog I had at home. And he was killed as it was told in the book. But of course it sounds much better to answer that Barabbas symbolizes the innocence of Clara, so that's the explanation I give when somebody asks.

Maybe the most important reason for writing is to

prevent the erosion of time, so that memories will not be blown away by the wind. Write to register history, and name each thing. Write what should not be forgotten. But then, why write novels? Probably because I come from Latin America, a land of crazy, illuminated people, of geological and political cataclysms — a land so large and profound, so beautiful and frightening, that only novels can describe its fascinating complexity.

A novel is like a window, open to an infinite landscape. In a novel we can put all the interrogations, we can register the most extravagant, evil, obscene, incredible or magnificent facts — which, in Latin America, are not hyperbole, because that is the dimension of our reality. In a novel we can give an illusory order to chaos. We can find the key to the labyrinth of history. We can make excursions into the past, to try to understand the present and dream the future. In a novel we can use everything: testimony, chronicle, essay, fantasy, legend, poetry and other devices that might help us to decode the mysteries of our world and discover our true identity.

For a writer who nourishes himself or herself on images and passions, to be born in a fabulous continent is a privilege. In Latin America we don't have to stretch our imaginations. Critics in Europe and the

United States often stare in disbelief at Latin American books, asking how the authors dare to invent those incredible lies of young women who fly to heaven wrapped in linen sheets; of black emperors who build fortresses with cement and the blood of emasculated bulls; of outlaws who die of hunger in the Amazon with bags full of emeralds on their backs; of ancient tyrants who order their mothers to be flogged naked in front of the troops and modern tyrants who order children to be tortured in front of their parents; of hurricanes and earthquakes that turn the world upside down; of revolutions made with machetes, bullets, poems and kisses; of hallucinating landscapes where reason is lost.

It is very hard to explain to critics that these things are not a product of our pathological imaginations. They are written in our history; we can find them every day in our newspapers. We hear them in the streets; we suffer them frequently in our own lives. It is impossible to speak of Latin America without mentioning violence. We inhabit a land of terrible contrasts and we have to survive in times of great violence.

Contrast and violence, two excellent ingredients for literature, although for us, citizens of that reality, life is always suspended from a very fragile thread.

The first, the most naked and visible form of violence is the extreme poverty of the majority, in contrast with the extreme wealth of the very few. In my continent two opposite realities coexist. One is a legal face, more or less comprehensible and with a certain pretension to dignity and civilization. The other is a dark and tragic face, which we do not like to show but which is always threatening us. There is an apparent world and a real world — nice neighborhoods where blond children play on their bicycles and servants walk elegant dogs, and other neighborhoods, of slums and garbage, where dark children play naked with hungry mutts. There are offices of marble and steel where young executives discuss the stock market, and forgotten villages where people still live and die as they did in the Middle Ages. There is a world of fiction created by the official discourse, and another world of blood and pain and love, where we have struggled for centuries.

In Latin America we all survive on the borderline of those two realities. Our fragile democracies exist as long as they don't interfere with imperialist interests. Most of our republics are dependent on submissiveness. Our institutions and laws are inefficient. Our armed forces often act as mercenaries for a privileged social group that pays tribute to transnational enterprises. We are living in the worst economic, political and social crisis since the conquest of America by the Spaniards. There are hardly two or three leaders in the whole continent. Social inequality is greater every day, and to avoid an outburst of public rancor, repression also rises day by day. Crime, drugs, misery and ignorance are present in every Latin American country, and the military is an immediate threat to society and civil governments. We try to keep straight faces while our feet are stuck in a swamp of violence, exploitation, corruption, the terror of the state and the terrorism of those who take arms against the status quo.

But Latin America is also a land of hope and friendship and love. Writers navigate in these agitated waters. They don't live in ivory towers; they cannot remove themselves from this brutal reality. In such circumstances there is no time and no wish for narcissistic literature. Very few of our writers contemplate their navel in self-centered monologue. The majority want desperately to communicate.

I feel that writing is an act of hope, a sort of communion with our fellow men. The writer of good will carries a lamp to illuminate the dark corners. Only that, nothing more — a tiny beam of light to show some hidden aspect of reality, to help decipher and understand it and thus to initiate, if possible, a change in the conscience of some readers. This kind of writer is not seduced by the mermaid's voice of celebrity or tempted by exclusive literary circles. He has both feet planted firmly on the ground and walks hand in hand with the people in the streets. He knows that the lamp is very small and the shadows are immense. This makes him humble.

But just as we should not believe that literature gives us any sort of power, neither should we be paralyzed by false modesty. We should continue to write in spite of the bruises and the vast silence that frequently surrounds us. A book is not an end in itself; it is only a way to touch someone — a bridge extended across a space of loneliness and obscurity — and sometimes it is a way of winning other people to our causes.

I believe in certain principles and values: love, generosity, justice. I know that sounds old-fashioned. However, I believe in those values so firmly that I'm willing to provoke some scornful smiles. I'm sure we have the capacity to build a more gentle world — that doing so is our only alternative, because our present equilibrium is very fragile. In literature, we have been told, optimism is dangerous; it flirts with simplicity and is an insurrection against the sacred laws of reason and good taste. But I don't belong to that group of desperate intellectuals. Despair is a paralyzing feeling. It only benefits our enemies.

My second novel, *Of Love and Shadows*, tells about the *desaparecidos*, "the disappeared ones." It's based on a political massacre that took place in Chile in 1973 during the military coup that put an end to 150 years of democracy. The novel denounces repression and the impunity of the murderers, and it had a warm reception from most readers and critics. But it also drew some strong attacks. Some said it was too political and sentimental and not very objective, as if one could be objective about the crimes of a dictatorship. Maybe these critics would have forgiven me, as other writers have been forgiven, if the book had only been a story of horror and bitterness. They didn't like the fact that in the novel solidarity and hope prevail over death and torture. If the main characters, Irene and Francisco, had died in a torture chamber, or at least if the violent experiences they endured had drowned them in despair and destroyed forever their capacity to love and to dream, these critics might have been more tolerant. Evidently it's hard to accept in literature that love can be stronger than hatred, although it frequently is in life.

If my books are going to be classified as political, I hope readers will find out that they are not political for ideological reasons only, but for other, more subtle considerations. They are political precisely because Alba Trueba, in *The House of the Spirits*, who has been raped, tortured and mutilated, is able to reconcile herself with life; because Irene and Francisco, in *Of Love and Shadows*, make love in spite of terror; because in my third novel, *Eva Luna*, Eva defeats the odds of her fate with generosity and candor; because these characters search for truth and have the courage to risk their lives.

I suppose I have the secret ambition to become a great writer, to be able to create stories that will resist the passage of time and the judgment of history. Yes, I know, it's terribly pretentious! But I'm more interested in touching my readers — as many of them as possible — on a spiritual and emotional level. To do this from a feminine point of view is a beautiful challenge in the society I live in. The political literature that some women writers have begun to create is so revolutionary that no wonder many critics are scared. Women are questioning the set of values that have sustained human society since the first apes stood on their feet and raised their eyes to the sky. After centuries of silence, women are taking by assault the exclusive male club of literature. Some women have done it before, of course, struggling against formidable obstacles. But now half of the novels published in Europe and the United States are written by women. Our sisters are using the cutting edge of words to change the rules we have always had to obey. Until now, humankind has organized itself according to certain principles that are considered part of nature: we are all born (it has been said) with some original sin; we are basically evil, and without the strict control of religion and laws we would devour each other like cannibals; authority, repression and punishment are necessary to keep us in line. According to these theories, the best proof of our perverse nature is that the world is what it is — a round rock lost in the cosmic nightmare, where abuse, war, inequality and hatred prevail.

But a small group of women and young men are now making the most astonishing statements. Fortunately, most of them work in the best universities, so even if they are only a few, their voices have great impact. These people are questioning everything, starting with our own image as human beings. Until now, men have decided the destiny of this suffering planet, imposing ambition, power and individualism as virtues. (They don't admit this, of course; it is more eloquent to speak of peace and cooperation.)

These values are also present in literature. Critics, most of them men, as you probably can guess, have determined what is good in literature — what is valuable or artistic, according to our aesthetic, intellectual and moral patterns — leaving aside the feminine half of the human race, whose opinions on this or any other matter don't interest them.

I think it's time to revise this situation. But it is not the Old Guard who will do it. It will be done by women and by young men who have nothing to lose and therefore have no fear.

In the process of analyzing books, critics have exalted all kinds of literary experiments, some of them quite unbearable. How many books have you tried to read lately and haven't gotten past page fifteen because they were simply boring? Flamboyant literary techniques win awards even though the subject is deplorable. The worst vices are glorified if the writing is elegant. Lies, bitterness and arrogance are forgiven if the language is original and the author already has his laurels. Pessimism is in fashion.

But many novels that don't fit that pattern are now being written by women and by some brave men, not all of them young — for example, García Márquez, who wrote that incredible and sentimental book *Love in the Time of Cholera,* which is a sort of magnificent soap opera about two old people who fall in love, and they love each other for eighty years. It's wonderful.

Those writers are shaking the literary world nowadays because they propose a completely new set of values. They don't accept the old rules anymore. They are willing to examine everything — to invent all over again and to express other ethical and aesthetic values; not always to replace the prevailing ones, but to complement them. It's not a question of changing male chauvinism for militant feminism, but of giving both women and men a chance to become better people and to share the heavy burden of this planet. I believe that this is the true political literature of our time.

All political systems, even revolutions, have been created and directed by men, always within the patriarchal regime. Important philosophical movements have tried to change man and society, but without touching the basis of human relations — that is, inequality of the sexes. Men writers of all periods have written political literature, from *Utopia* to parody, but feminine values have been scorned and women have been denied a voice to express them.

Now, finally, women are breaking the rule of silence and raising a strong voice to question the world. This is a cataclysm. It is a new literature that dares to be optimistic — to speak of love in opposition to pornography, of compassion against cruelty. It is a literature that's not afraid of colloquial language, of being sentimental if necessary; a literature that searches the spiritual dimension of reality, that accepts the unknown and the unexplainable, confusion and terror; a literature that has no answers, only questions; a literature that doesn't invent history or try to explain the world solely with reason, but also seeks knowledge through feelings and imagination. Maybe, this literature says, it's not true that we are perverse and evil. Maybe the idea of original sin is just a terrible mistake. Maybe we are not here to be punished, because the gods love us and are willing to give us a chance to decipher the clues and trace new paths.

The effect of these books is hard to measure, because the old instruments are no longer useful. Probably the strongest literature being written nowadays is by those who stand unsheltered by the system: blacks, Indians, homosexuals, exiles and, especially, women — the crazy people of the world, who dare to believe in their own force. We dare to think that humanity is not going to destroy itself, that we have the capacity to reach an agreement, not only for survival but also to achieve happiness. That is why we write — as an act of human solidarity and commitment to the future. We want to change the rules, even if we won't live long enough to see the results. We have to make real revolutions of the spirit, of values, of life. And to do so we have to begin dreaming them.

So I will continue to write: about two lovers embracing in the moonlight, near an abandoned mine where they have found the bodies of fifteen peasants, murdered by the military. Or about raped women and tortured men and families who sell themselves as slaves because they are starving. And also — why not? — about golden sunsets and loving mothers and poets who die of love. I want to tell stories and say, for example, that I care more for the free man than the free enterprise, more for solidarity than charity. I want to say that it's more important for me to share than to compete. And I want to write about the necessary changes in Latin America that will enable us to rise from our knees after five centuries of humiliations.

Much skill will be needed to write about these things eloquently. But with patience and hard work I hope to acquire that skill. I suppose I'm being very ambitious. Well, most writers are, even women writers.

Now, for whom do I write?
When I face a clean sheet of paper, I don't think of a large audience or of the people who would raise

their knives to cut me in pieces. If I did, terror would paralyze me. Instead, when I write, a benevolent image comes to my mind — that of Alexandra Jorquera, a young woman who lives in Chile whom I scarcely know. She has read my books so many times that she can repeat paragraphs by heart. In fact, she knows them better than I do. She quotes me and I don't know she's quoting me. Once she told me that she had discovered in my books the history of Chile that is denied by the official textbooks of the dictatorship — the forbidden and secret history that nevertheless is still alive in the memories of most Chileans.

This is the best compliment my work has ever received. For the sake of this girl I am very demanding with my writing. Sometimes, tempted by the beauty of a sentence, I am about to betray the truth, and then Alexandra comes to my mind and I remember that she, and others like her, don't deserve that. At other times I'm too explicit, too near the pamphlet. But then I step back, thinking she doesn't deserve that either — to be underestimated. And when I feel helpless against brutality and suffering, her candid face brings back my strength. All writers should have a reader like her, waiting for their words. They would never feel lonely, and their work would have a new and shining dimension.

In Latin America today, 50 percent of the population is illiterate. Among those who can read and write, only very few can buy books, and among those who can buy books, very few have the habit of reading. What, then, is the importance of a book in Latin America? None, would be the reasonable answer. But it's not exactly that way. For some strange reason, the written word has a tremendous impact in that illiterate continent. The totalitarian regimes have persecuted, tortured, sent into exile and murdered many writers. This is not an accident; dictators don't make mistakes in these details. They know that a book can be dangerous for them. In our countries most of the press is controlled by private enterprises or by inefficient governments. Eduardo Galeano, the great writer from Uruguay, puts it bluntly: "Almost all mass media promote a colonialistic culture, which justifies the unjust organization of the world as a result of the legitimate victory of the best — that is, the strongest. They lie about the past and about reality. They propose a lifestyle which postulates consumerism as an alternative to communism, which exalts crime as achievement, lack of scruples as virtue, and selfishness as a natural requirement."

What can writers do against this persistent and powerful message? The first thing we should try to do is write clearly. Not simply — that only works with soap advertising; we don't have to sacrifice aesthetics for the sake of ethics. On the contrary, only if we are able to say it beautifully can we be convincing. Most readers are perfectly able to appreciate subtleties and poetic twists and symbols and metaphors. We should not write with a paternalistic attitude, as if readers were simple-minded, but we should also beware of elaborate and unnecessary ornamentation, which frequently hides a lack of ideas. It has been said that we Spanish-speaking people have the vice of empty words, that we need six hundred pages to say what would be better told in fifty.

The opportunity to reach a large number of readers is a great responsibility. Unfortunately, it is hard for a book to stand against the message of the mass media; it's an unfair battle. Writers should therefore look for other forms of expressing their thoughts, avoiding the prejudice that only in books can they make literature. All means are legitimate, not only the cultivated language of academia but also the direct language of journalism, the mass language of radio, television and the movies, the poetic language of popular songs and the passionate language of talking face to face with an audience. These are all forms of literature. Let us be clever and use every opportunity to introduce ourselves in the mass media and try to change them from within.

In Venezuela, José Ignacio Cabrujas, a playwright and novelist, one of the most brilliant intellectuals of the country, writes soap operas. These shows are the most important cultural phenomenon in Latin America. Some people watch three or four a day, so you can imagine how important that kind of writing is. Cabrujas doesn't elude reality. His soap operas show a world of contrasts. He presents problems such as abortion, divorce, machismo, poverty and crime. The result is quite different from "Dynasty." But it's also very successful.

I tried to put some of that soap opera stuff in *Eva Luna*, because I'm fascinated by that version of reality. The ladies on TV wear false eyelashes at eleven in the morning. The difference between rich and poor is that the rich wear cocktail gowns all the time and the poor have their faces painted black. They all go blind or become invalids and then they recover. Just like real life!

Many of the most important Latin American writers have been journalists, and they go back to it frequently because they are aware that their words in a newspaper or on the radio reach an audience that their books can never touch. Others write for the theater or the movies, or write lyrics for popular songs. All means are valid if we want to communicate and don't presume to be writing only for an educated elite or for literary prizes.

In Latin America a book is almost a luxury. My hairdresser calls me Dr. Allende because I usually carry a book, and she probably thinks that a doctorate is the minimum prerequisite for such an extravagance. In Chile a novel of three hundred pages can cost the equivalent of a laborer's monthly wages. In some other countries — like Haiti, for example — 85 percent of the population is illiterate. Elsewhere in Latin America, nothing is published in the Indian languages of the majority. Many publishers have been ruined by the economic crisis, and the price of books imported from Spain is very high.

However, we should not despair. There is some hope for the spirit. Literature has survived even in the worst conditions. Political prisoners have written stories on cigarette paper. In the wars of Central America, little soldiers, fourteen years old, write poetry in their school notebooks. The Pieroa Indians, those who haven't yet been exterminated by the genocide being carried out against the aborigines of the Amazon, have published some legends in their language.

In my continent, writers often have more prestige than they do in any other part of the world. Some writers are considered witch doctors, or prophets, as if they were illuminated by a sort of natural wisdom. Jorge Amado has to spend part of the year away from Brazil in order to write, because people crowd into his house seeking advice. Mario Vargas-Llosa directs the opposition to Alan Garcia's government in Peru. García Márquez is a frequent middleman for Central American presidents. In Venezuela, Arturo Uslar Pietri is consulted on issues like corruption and oil. These writers have interpreted their reality and told it to the world. Some of them even have the gift of foretelling the future and put in words the hidden thoughts of their people, which of course include social and political problems, because it is impossible to write in a crystal bubble, disregarding the conditions of their continent.

No wonder Latin American novels are so often accused of being political.

For whom do I write, finally? Certainly for myself. But mainly for others, even if there are only a few. For those who have no voice and for those who are kept in silence. For my children and my future grandchildren. For Alexandra Jorquera and others like her. I write for you.

And why do I write? García Márquez once said that he writes so that his friends will love him more. I think I write so that people will love each other more. Working with words is a beautiful craft, and in my continent, where we still have to name all things one by one, it has a rich and profound meaning.

CHARLES McCARRY

A Strip of
Exposed Film

IT'S VERY GOOD to be back in this great library, where I spent so many happy hours as a young man. Thirty-eight years ago this spring I wrote a poem about James Joyce in the Reading Room that won the heart of a Greenwich Village girl for an entire afternoon. I lost her about five o'clock when I wrote a sequel that quoted Molly Bloom's famous words: "Yes I said yes I will Yes."

In those days I supported my poetry, which was unpublished, by washing dishes three nights a week at Sardi's. It was a very good job. I got it through a friend who was also an unpublished poet, and, more important, was a busboy. It paid $6.80 a night and two meals. The food was very good. My room on Christopher Street — hotplate in the bathroom, world at the doorstep — cost $6 a week. So I had about $14 left over to buy coffee for Greenwich Village girls and other necessities. Later I gave up dishwashing and started to write short stories so that I could continue to write poetry, and then I started to write articles so that I could write short stories so that I could write poetry, and finally books, so that I could write articles so that I could write short stories so that I could write poetry. This process has led me back here, after all these years — I'm still an unpublished poet — and I have to tell you that it's a dream come true that nine of my books are sitting on a shelf somewhere in the stacks upstairs, not too far away from Melville.

I'm here tonight because I'm very amiable when I'm writing. When my children were little they used to wait for me to come out of the room in which I wrote and they'd say, "Daddy, can I have a horse?" or "Can I have a new bicycle?" — my son John once asked for a goat — and I would always say, "Uh-huh," and they'd go to their mother and say, "Daddy said I can have a goat." And she would say, "Well, you know perfectly well that your father is writing, and he doesn't know what he's saying."

When I was invited to give a talk here on the politi-

cal novel, I was writing a book, so I said, "Uh-huh."
The fact is, I'm not quite sure what a political novel is.

The best novels, I believe, are about ordinary things:
love, betrayal, death, trust, loneliness, marriage, fatherhood.

On the basis of my experience with the people who
run the world I'd have to say that it's a mistake to
believe that somewhere there is a hidden room, and
inside that room there is a vault, and inside that vault
there is a book containing the secret of life. That belief in the hidden room, the vault and the book containing the secret of life is, of course, the basis of
political conviction. Even more, it's the basis of the
political novel. But as Oscar Wilde observed, "The
mystery of the world is the visible, not the invisible."
The visible is the territory of the novel.

Around 1962 I wrote a play about a young woman
who obtains an abortion without telling her lover that
she is going to do so. It was this situation — the betrayal of trust — that interested me; it certainly never
occurred to me that I was making a political point. At
that time abortion was illegal almost everywhere in
Christendom, on religious grounds. The penalty in
Spain, where the action of the play takes place, was
life in prison.

It was unusual to deal with the subject on the stage, and I didn't think the piece had much chance of being produced. However, my agent showed the script to a producer in London who was putting on avant garde plays in the East End. The producer flew over to France, where my wife and I and our children were living at the time, to talk about it. We met for lunch at Lasserre, a very expensive restaurant in Paris. Everything went well. While eating his appetizer and drinking his white wine the producer praised the structure, the action and the dialogue of my play. Then, halfway through the red wine and the meat, he suddenly became very agitated. His face filled with color.

Finally he said, "Do you read the English papers?" I said, "Yes, on Sunday." And he said, "Well, then you must know that a bill to legalize abortion has been before the House of Commons and everyone is for it. How do you expect me to produce a play that says abortion makes people sad?" I said, "It *does* make some people sad." "Of course it does," he replied. "But you've picked the wrong bloody time to say so." He overturned his wine glass, threw down his napkin and rushed out of the restaurant. And stuck me with the check.

I understood that he had flown to Paris not to produce my play but because my play had made him so angry that he wanted to point out the flaws in my political consciousness.

Even if you aren't writing for political reasons, the political climate at a given time has a great deal to do with what you can get away with. The Horatio Alger books, which are political novels in a very pure and simple form, wouldn't have made the same splash in any time but their own. André Malraux's *Man's Fate*, arguably the most admired political novel of the first half of the twentieth century, was also published at exactly the right moment, in 1933.

Anna Karenina, on the other hand, might as well have been published in 1975, or 1775, as in 1875. Anna is immortal because we see her in ourselves. But nobody like Horatio Alger's noble urchins or Malraux's noble assassin ever existed on this planet except in the mind of an idealist.

And that, of course, is the difficulty. It's possible, if you have a political point of view, to see all writing in political terms. In the Book of Exodus, for example, God is clearly talking politics when He says to Moses, "I will be an enemy to your enemies and an adversary to your adversaries. . . . I will drive them out before you little by little until you . . . take possession of the land." *Pride and Prejudice* is about the politics of marriage. *The Sun Also Rises* is about the politics of friendship. The relationship between Huckleberry Finn and Jim is an examination of the most profound political question in the history of the United States: slavery. *The Adventures of Huckleberry Finn* clearly provides all the evidence needed that a political novel can be a work of art. But the danger exists — because when you write a political novel you're writing what you believe instead of what you know — that you will produce something other than art.

I grew up during the Great Depression in the Berkshire hills of Massachusetts, in a small, isolated town. There was plenty of politics there, past and present. Before the Civil War, John Brown, the celebrated terrorist, had taught in the local school. The school is no longer in operation, but when I went there it had two rooms, with a row of desks for each of the eight grades. A library was attached to the school, but it was open only on Tuesday afternoons. However, if I finished my work early, as I usually did, my teacher, Miss Addie Dyer — may her name be remembered — would sometimes give me the key and let me go into the library and read all by myself. There was no heat, so I would put on my coat and hat and mittens and sit on the floor with James Fenimore

Cooper in my lap. You have to be a born reader to turn pages with your mittens on. It was there that I read a book that I now realize was the very model of a political novel — a book about life in a disputed territory and the struggle of a despised minority to establish a homeland in the face of its enemy's overwhelming military strength. One day the hero of the book, then still a boy, comes home to find his house burned, his father and brothers mutilated and murdered, and his mother and sisters raped and also dead. Radicalized by this experience, he becomes a terrorist, obsessed with the struggle against the oppressor — obsessed with revenge. He renounces all personal considerations and, working always alone, becomes such a remorseless operative that the enemy gives him a resonant code name, Deathwind.

The fierce struggle between the two sides, which is cultural as well as political and territorial, goes on for years. Deathwind is opposed by an enemy leader who is nearly his equal in skill and ferocity. Our hero wants to kill this man above all others, but he is never able to penetrate his security. In middle age the terrorist adopts a young man as his successor and trains him in his secret skills. Between missions the younger man gives way to his emotions and falls in love with a young woman. The enemy leader, seeing the opportunity this provides to lay hands on Deathwind, abducts the girl. Deathwind and the girl's lover rescue her, but the young man is captured, tortured and killed. Deathwind, lying in ambush and with revenge in his grasp at last, is on the point of assassinating the enemy leader when the latter performs an act that makes the terrorist realize that his enemy has been secretly converted to the ideology of Deathwind's people. The truth and justice of their cause has conquered the enemy's soul. For the first time in his life Deathwind stays his hand when in the presence of the enemy and does not kill.

The book I've just described is *The Spirit of the Border* by Zane Grey. The disputed territory was the bottomland along the Ohio River below what is now Wheeling, West Virginia; the cruel enemy were the Iroquoian tribes who lived along the river; the terrorist was an Indian fighter named Lou Wetzel, known to the Indians as Atalang, or Deathwind; and this implacable terrorist's ideology was, of course, Christianity. Zane Grey was a highly professional writer, possessed of a clear political vision. But he wrote the same book over and over again. The plot never varied, the characters changed nothing but their names. He had a message to deliver — the triumph of white Christian civilization was the will of God — and he developed a very good vehicle for delivering it.

If *The Spirit of the Border* were published today as a story of Afghanistan or Israel or Nicaragua, as it easily could be merely by changing the locale and the names and the vocabulary of the characters, it would find an enthusiastic readership. But it still wouldn't be a novel. It would be what it was to begin with: propaganda.

The propagandist sees things as he thinks they should be. The novelist must see things as they are, because his purpose is to record and illuminate human experience. The goal of politics is to alter human nature, and often politics substitutes a system of delusions for reality. Joseph Brodsky, who has had some experience of politics, recently commented on this question: "Literature is a far more ancient and viable thing than any social formation or state," he said. "A writer should care about one thing — the language. To write well: that is his duty. That is his only duty. The rest is an attempt to subordinate the writer to some statesman's purpose." The novelist can't be a believer, because he must be a heartless observer.

The real "invisible government," I sometimes think, is the system of attitudes and beliefs that causes us to see things that are not there. To go through life with this Iago whispering in one's ear is not only very bad for Desdemona's health; it's not very good for one's peace of mind. The writer's virtue consists of saving himself for the reader. A novel is a collaboration between the writer and the reader — a strip of exposed film that must be developed in the consciousness of many, many readers. A piece of writing does not become a novel until this process takes place in the minds of those readers, who compare the characters and the imaginary world of the novel to their own experience of life and, in talking about the book with their friends, become drawn into the novel's atmosphere. The writing is only part of it; the reading is the other part. A book that comes to the reader entire, not requiring this collaboration — this meeting between the writer, the characters and the reader — is not a novel. It may be brilliant, it may be entertaining, it may be uplifting, it may be moral, it may even change your life, but it's another breed of cat.

As a general rule I believe that the things we do on impulse turn out better than the things we do by calculation. In literary terms, then, it's better to be a Balzac than a Flaubert. Not that this is really a matter of choice; a novelist must write what he has lived. In *The Summing Up* Somerset Maugham remarked that he had never written an autobiography because in one way or another he had used everything that had ever happened to him in his fiction. Maugham may have done this in a more deliberate and conscious way than some other writers, and he made many enemies as a result. They persist even after his death. The new edition of *The Oxford Companion to English Literature*, for example, accuses him of using, almost verbatim, intimate details from the life stories of people who invited him to their homes. No doubt this was a breach of etiquette. But one wonders what Maugham's hosts thought he was going to do with the secrets they volunteered to tell him on those steamy nights in Malaya. Presumably they knew he was a writer when they asked him to stay. He could no more control his curiosity or his pen than a werewolf can stop the hair from growing on his forehead when the moon is full.

In any case, truth in life and truth in fiction are not the same. How the one becomes the other is the chief mystery of literature. Certainly I have never fully understood it, either as a writer or as a reader. A man I used to work with overseas has told me that he likes the parts I make up in my novels better than the parts he remembers from real life. I was surprised that he remembered which was which, because I have a lot of trouble with that. The fact is, I don't really know what I'm doing on the conscious level when I write. I've never kept a diary or a notebook and I've never written anything from an outline, not even a nonfiction book. I just think about a character and a situation for twenty or thirty years, and when the first line of the narrative comes into my head — the one in my new book is "As soon as the candles were lit at the wedding feast, Henry Harding asked his daughter Fanny to sing" — I sit down and let the characters write the book. Usually this doesn't take very long; the writing, after all, has been going on in the unconscious for decades. It's just a matter of transcribing it. The book that emerges may be one of four or five or six that I've long had in mind, and I never know which one is going to be ready first.

As an editor I've worked with a lot of writers — famous ones as well as journeymen. This has led me to the conclusion that far more writers are made than born. But most of the good ones are born. This inborn ability to write, like athletic ability, deserves no credit or admiration. Writing is work like any other work — although, in my case at least, it's ten times harder than anything else I've ever done.

Most writers discover early that the gift, the mere ability to string words together, is not enough. That's why so many of them live so foolishly, because they know they've got to have material. By the time I was twenty-three I had written the three novels that every writer has in him at that age — a novel about child-hood, a novel about star-crossed love, and the novel I didn't yet know enough to write. I realized that I didn't have the material, so I gave up fiction and went out into the world to learn about life. For the next fifteen years I didn't write a word of fiction except that play about abortion and one short story that I wrote on a bet and was surprised to see published in *The Saturday Evening Post.*

At the end of the fifteen years I knew so much about life that the last thing I wanted to do was de-scribe it. And it was five more years before I tried another novel — *The Miernik Dossier*, in 1972. Since then I've been writing one long novel about an Ameri-can family called Christopher. This work now amounts to six volumes hopping across three centuries. A lot of gaps remain to be filled, and if I live long enough I hope to deal with those. I haven't written the parts in any particular order, and I don't think it's neces-sary to read them in any particular order.

Maugham said that he intended *Of Human Bond-age* to be one long telegram to the reader. I suppose what I've been doing is writing a series of long letters to you all. One of these letters, *The Bride of the Wilderness*, takes place between Easter 1699 and Easter 1701. It's the story of the Christophers' most remote American ancestor, an English girl of seventeen who comes to the Connecticut River Valley in Massachusetts during the War of the Spanish Succession, or Queen Anne's War, as it was called in the American colonies.

The French and the British in North America fought this war mainly with Indian proxies — the British using the Mohawks and other Iroquoian tribes, and the French using the Algonquin people, of whom the Abenaki Indians were the most important. One of the scenes in my novel is a description of an attack by the Abenakis on an English settlement. It's an extremely violent passage. My wife, who has been my first and best reader for thirty-six years, turned to me after she read it in manuscript and said, "Where in the world did that come from?" Interesting question. The factual background — what the Abenakis looked like, what they wore, the weapons and tactics they used, their rituals and beliefs, the way they treated their captives, the way they dressed their hair — came from scholarly sources and from contemporary accounts written by people who had been captured by these Indians. The research that uncovered these details was very evocative in political terms. I was surprised by the similarities between the seventeenth century and the twentieth. Both were eras of great faith and great violence. The resemblance struck me as so strong that I put a tag on the book from Horace: "Change the names and the story is about you."

"Religion," wrote the British historian G. M. Trevelyan, referring to the seventeenth century, "was then associated with the rack, the stake, the burning town, the massacre of women and children, the hate that never dies, the wrong that can never be avenged." Substitute "politics" for "religion" and you have a fair description of our own times. The Thirty Years' War, in which one single judge burned ten thousand witches and whole provinces in Germany were depopulated and laid waste, would look familiar to twentieth-century peasants who are the victims of the Forty Years' War that has been going on in Asia, Africa and Latin America since the end of World War II.

In this kinship of violence and faith across the ages I found a possible answer to my wife's question. The real sources of my narrative of an Indian attack in Massachusetts at the turn of the seventeenth century had come to me, I realized, in twentieth-century Japan. In *The Bride of the Wilderness* a young Frenchman is drowned on the way to the attack. The Abenakis, worried that he will become a ghost, try to revive him by holding his body over a campfire. Then they break his limbs, put him onto a pack frame, carry him into the woods and hide his body in a tree. Now I realized (though I didn't realize it when I was writing it) that this scene came from stories that guides in the Japan Alps had told me about their early experiences with mountain rescues in the years between World Wars I and II — in particular, an account of how they had found the body of a member of the imperial family who had been buried by an avalanche. "When we dug away the snow," the guide said, "the prince looked as if he were asleep. We had never seen anyone with such beautiful skin and we were afraid to touch him." They held this prince's frozen body over a fire in an attempt to revive him. Finally the strongest man among them, whose name was Ohtani, tied the body onto his pack frame and carried it down the mountain through the snow. It took him two days because he had no skis and the snow was ten feet deep. "Of course," Ohtani said, "I had to break his limbs in order to fold him into a bundle, so he must be very uncomfortable in the next world."

The episode in my novel, as I said, is full of violence: people are shot, hatcheted, strangled, stabbed and burned to death. All this is viewed with equanimity by both sides, as something that is part of the natural order. This, too, comes from events I witnessed in Asia, but especially from a conversation I had in Japan some years ago. I had been climbing in the Japan Alps. Out of the blue, my wife and I were invited to visit the head man of a village called Nodaira. His name was Toyomi Yamagishi. The same twenty families had been living in this very remote village since the twelfth century; the first road had been built only thirty years earlier. Before that everything that went into the village and came out of the village went in or came out on the back of a human being.

We were invited for ten in the morning, the usual Japanese hour for such affairs. The village was very high, above the altitude at which you can grow rice; you can only grow millet. It was at the end of a narrow mountain road. The snowbanks were ten or twelve feet and in some places fifteen feet high. Yamagishi's was a typical Japanese house despite its location — thin walls, sliding doors. It was bitterly cold inside — colder, it seemed, than it had been outside. We all sat around a table that had a blanket on it and a charcoal brazier under it, so that your lower body was warm enough and you warmed your upper body by drinking whiskey and sake at ten in the morning.

A feast had been laid out: besides whiskey and sake, there was beer, cookies of all kinds, pretzels, ice cream, a box of cornflakes. Yamagishi's wife, a tiny woman no more than four and half feet tall, served us in the Japanese style, on her knees. After we had drunk green tea and eaten, Yamagishi, who had been silent up to that point, began to speak. He spoke in a recitative style, somewhat like the narration of a Noh play or a Bunraku puppet theater performance, except that he was speaking modern Japanese so that we could understand what he was saying.

He said he had invited us to his house because he had never met an American and had wanted to ever since World War II. We chatted a little about the history of the village and about the life that he and the other villagers had led before the war. He said it had been a life of ceaseless toil. As a child he had only rarely seen the faces of his parents because they worked every day from dark to dark, leaving the hut before he woke and returning after he was asleep. He had had no children of his own because he wanted to avoid this sadness in his own life. I remarked that I had grown up on a farm and knew how hard that life could be. "I'm sorry," he said, "but you do not know. Human beings are not beasts of burden in America."

Yamagishi then told us about his life during the war. He had been drafted in 1944, at the age of forty, and sent to Osaka to guard the emperor's forest. Then the Americans took Saipan and the B-29s came. "The Americans burned the forest with incendiary bombs, so it was not necessary to guard it any longer," he said. "I became a firefighter. The Americans would drop incendiary bombs to set the city on fire, and when we went to fight the fires they would wait until we were very busy and then they would come over with other B-29s and drop antipersonnel bombs and kill the firemen. I thought, 'The Americans are very clever.' Then, after the whole city had been destroyed, a single B-29 flew over Osaka and dropped not bombs but hundreds of little parachutes. When these parachutes landed we saw that a gift was tied to each — a mirror, a harmonica, a fountain pen. The Japanese people had lost nearly everything in the bombing and they were very glad to have these gifts from the Americans. They ran to get them, and when they touched them they exploded in their hands, blowing off fingers and blinding people. I thought, 'The Americans are not only clever; they are ruthless. We have lost the war.' "

Yamagishi said, "Your ships came and shelled us. The bombers kept on also, every day. I was assigned to train people to fight the Americans when they invaded. We showed women and children how to make spears from bamboo. Every Japanese was prepared to die defending the homeland. Then the atom bombs were dropped on Hiroshima and Nagasaki. The emperor's voice came over loudspeakers in the streets. He told us we must surrender. No one had ever heard his voice before, and to us it was the voice of God. But our commanding officer said, 'No! We must kill the Americans! He is no true emperor if he tells the Japanese to surrender.' Nevertheless we obeyed the emperor, and I came back to this village. All the younger sons of every family — all twenty families — had been killed in the war. Only old men and women were left to do the work. I thought we would starve to death. But as you see, we did not.

"Now," the old Japanese said, "I will tell you why I invited you here. It is because I have something to say to you, and to all Americans." He was out of breath and his face was full of color from the whiskey he had drunk, and I thought, "Well, here it comes."

Yamagishi said, "Thank you. Thank you for defeating Japan. If you Americans had not done so, this village would be as it always was. The militarists would never have let us have democracy. But the Americans built the road; my nephews and nieces have cars and television sets, and they see their children every day. And because they have eaten American things like milk and vegetables and fruit, instead of the millet and pickles *we* had to eat, they are tall and beautiful like Americans instead of short and homely like me and my wife." He bowed and said, "Thank you." I realized, to my surprise, and in spite of everything I believed about the morality of bombing civilians, that the U.S. Air Force had won Yamagishi's heart and mind by pitilessly destroying Osaka, Hiroshima and Nagasaki.

In one of my novels a political idealist asks Paul Christopher what he believes in. Christopher replies, "I believe in consequences." In the novel, as in politics and in life itself, you can't know what the consequences of any act will be until you come to the end.

MARGE PIERCY

Active in Time and History

I'M GOING TO start with a relevant poem of mine, called "And Whose Creature Am I?"

At times characters from my novels swarm through me,
children of my mind, and possess me as dybbuks.
My own shabby memories they have plucked and eaten
till sometimes I cannot remember my own sorrows.
In all that I value there is a core of mystery,
in the seed that wriggles its new roots into the soil
and whose pale head bursts the surface,
in the dance where our bodies merge and reassemble,
in the starving baby whose huge glazing eyes
burned into my bones, in the look that passes
between predator and prey before the death blow.

I know of what rags and bones and clippings
from frothing newsprint and poisonous glue

my structures are built. Yet these creatures
I have improvised like golem walk off and thrive.
Between one and two thirds of our lives we spend
in darkness, and the little lights we turn on
make little holes in that great thick rich void.
We are never done with knowing or with gnawing,
but under the saying is whispering, touching
and silence. Out of a given set of atoms
we cast and recast the holy patterns new.

I will first talk about what I perceive as a difference between writing poetry and writing fiction, as one who works equally hard and with equal commitment in both forms. Then I'll talk a little bit about the experience of writing fiction and what I consider the aim of this quaint activity.

My poetry appears to me at once more personal and more universal than my fiction. In my poems I speak mostly in my own persona or in a voice that's a public form of it, except for occasional poems in another character. Some poems come out of my own experiences and some issue from the energy of other people's experiences coming through me, but they are fused in the layers of my mind to a speaking voice.

I think of poetry as utterance that heals the psyche because of the way it uses verbal signs and symbols, sound and rhythm, memory and dream images, blending all the different kinds of knowing — the analytical and the synthetic, the rational and the prerational, the gestalt grasping of new and ancient configurations. For the moment of experiencing a poem we may be healed to our diverse selves, connecting thinking, feeling, seeing, remembering and dreaming — at least at that moment.

Fiction is as old a habit of our species as poetry. It goes back to telling a tale, the first perceptions of pattern, and fiction is still about pattern in human life. At its core it answers the question What then? And then? And then, and then? I've tried to figure out, coming into postmodern poetry and fiction, exactly why people have carried out these activities, what they were supposed to do, why I engage in them and why others should pay attention to what I produce.

Poetry is an art of time, as music is. Rhythms are measured against time; they are measures of time. A poem goes forward a beat at a time, the way dance does, step by step, phrase by phrase. But fiction is *about* time. First this, then that. Or this; and before it, *that* happened. Therefore this. From the perception of the seasons, of winter, spring, summer, fall, of the seasons of our lives, of the things that return and the things that don't return, of the drama of the searching and finding of the fruit, the seed, the root that sustains life; the looking and the hunting and the kill; the arc of the sex act; the climax of giving birth: these are the sources of the fictional intelligence. If you make such a choice — being kind to an old woman you meet on the road, marrying Bluebeard against all advice, apprenticing yourself to a witch — what follows?

Why do ordinary people read fiction? The most primitive answer is the most real: to get to the next page. To find out what happens next, and what happens after that; to find out how it all comes out.

That desire for finding a pattern of events still functions as a major hunger we bring to the novel — for not all happenings will satisfy us, but only the right ending, the proper disaster, or the proper reward, or the proper suspension. We want stories that help us to make sense of our lives. We want to see all this mess mean something, even if what we discover is a shape perhaps beautiful but not necessarily comforting.

In some ways the novel is the freest of forms. Nothing equivalent to the sonnet or the neoclassical play has ever been successfully imposed upon it. Its laws are inner and organic. The effects of a novel are tremendously subjective and partially moral. Questions like Do we like Anna Karenina? Can we be a little in love with Vronsky? Do we approve of Hester Prynne? Do we desire Heathcliff? all become relevant to how we experience a novel. If you look at Rodin's *Thinker*, it would be absurd to stop and wonder whether you would like him as a friend, or even whether you would like to spend an evening eating dinner with him in a restaurant. But with a novel such questions arise. Personal chemistry is always involved.

As I said, a novel is about time and patterns in time. It's not a simultaneous art, but one of transition and sequence. You can give the effect of simultaneity, but it's only created by illusion. A novel also takes time to read, so it involves much persuasion. You must persuade the reader to start reading — and continue reading. You have to persuade her not to put the book down on page 1 or page 100, or page 200, or page 700 — not to skip. Fiction is an art of constant persuasion. The use of suspense and one of the uses of identification with a protagonist is to make the reader go on reading and turning pages.

My novels feel very different to me, each a small world. A novel is something I inhabit for two or three years, like a marriage or a house. It owns me and I live inside it. When I'm writing a novel it preoccupies me and stains my life with its particular emotional coloration.

I start with a basic theme. Then I work on character. This is all preliminary to writing anything whatsoever. At this time I have a very basic, rough sense of plot. I work on character until I've compiled extensive notes and dossiers on the major characters and I'm very clear about their viewpoints — how each of them thinks and feels and senses and speaks and moves.

Then I work on plot. I figure the general plot line before I start. I know roughly the length of the book at this point, give or take fifty pages. As I write the rough draft, I work out details of the plot and invent the minor characters as I need them. Often some of them will develop into somewhat more important characters in future drafts.

What I know and don't know about the plot could be stated like this: About a third of the way through *Gone to Soldiers* Jacqueline and her mother have a serious fight, so Jacqueline storms out, not meaning to run away permanently. This keeps her away from home at a critical time: the night of the Grande Rafle, when twenty thousand French Jews (including five thousand children) were picked up by the French police, under instructions from the Gestapo, and taken to a rink used for bicycle races in the winter. There they were held for eight days without food or water. A great number of the children died. This was the first relay on the road to mass death.

Now I have to find a good reason to remove Jacqueline from her mother's flat in Paris because she has to survive. Naturally I would like it to be an absence that isn't accidental or contrived, something like: "Tonight, Maman, I will sleep at my girlfriend's." So I figure, with Jacqueline being nineteen in the hot summer of 1942 and out of college, because she's been forced out for being Jewish, I will give her a boyfriend. She will at this time begin sleeping with him. That fact, discovered by her mother, will get them into a huge argument and Jacqueline can storm out of the house. So Jacqueline has to have a boyfriend, who, to keep her out of danger that night, can't be Jewish. Now what sort of man would be indifferent at that time to the laws and pressure forbidding such an association? One of the *zazous*, the zoot-suiters of Paris, who defied the Nazis by wearing their hair long and greasy, listening to jazz and acting cool. Now we have Jacqueline's boyfriend Henri emerging, and the plot begins to fill in. This is an actual instance of problem solving from the first draft of *Gone to Soldiers*. That's how it works.

The first draft is always scary to me. I can't risk interrupting it for long or I may lose it. The momentum is important; there's a sense of pushing off from one side. It's like building the Verrazano Bridge from one side, hoping it won't fall in on the way. You don't know if you're going to make it.

Sometimes my identification with my characters becomes dangerous. I can lose myself in them until I have trouble functioning in my own life. For *Gone to Soldiers* I lived for seven years in World War II, and it's sort of weird. I can't sleep. Sometimes I can't get out of the character or the novel. These are the dangers of the first draft.

Between the first and second draft I look for structural flaws and work more on character. I do a lot of detailed plotting, and I generally accomplish whatever research wasn't finished before I began chapter one. A lot of research is useless for the first draft anyhow; it doesn't get incorporated even if you have all your facts on hand.

In the second draft I start paying serious attention to language. Some of the concern has solved itself already. Concentrating on theme and character goes a long way toward evolving the correct style for a subject, a story, a set of people.

As a political writer often I have a fair amount of research to do for a novel. For *Going Down Fast*, my first novel to be published, I had to understand the uses of urban renewal and the conglomeration of real estate and corporate powers that control cities, and I had to understand Chicago's history and politics. For *Woman on the Edge of Time* I had to research brain functions, psychosurgery, how it feels to be in a mental institution. A lot of studying was preliminary to thinking about a good future society. *Gone to Soldiers* has seven years of research on World War II behind it.

All my current research I keep in a database system in my computer. Everything — bibliography, notes from reading, interviews — goes into it. I can retrieve whatever I need for a particular section of a novel. *Gone to Soldiers* would have been impossible to finish in the time I had without computer technology. I would have drowned in notes.

I clip periodicals heavily. In fact, my house always has this yellowing glacier of newsprint creeping through the rooms at varying speeds. From 1964 through 1983, before I began using a computer, I had a fairly sophisticated hand-held system of notched cards. It was very nice but it took me hours to explain it to people — much longer to explain than to use. Now I just say I use the computer, and nobody wants to know how it works. It's like your refrigerator. If you put it in, you get it out. Put the milk in, get the milk out.

I like revision. It's work that has more play in it,

less spinning from the gut. By that point I know I can get through. The problems are large, perhaps, but a lot smaller than the horizon. I can get my mind around them.

Between the second and third draft — or, in a more complex book, between the third and fourth draft — I have the habit of circulating my manuscript to other people, usually anywhere from seven to ten people. Some are writers and some aren't. I ask for criticism. This is the time when I care a great deal for other opinions. I can accept or reject any reaction, but I need feedback on what works and what doesn't, on what others see when they look at the work. I often ask people who have a specific expertise to look over the entire novel, or sections of the novel, to see whether I've committed any obvious gaffes, or whether I've handled the jargon essential to one or more characters idiomatically.

I also try out the work politically at that point, asking old friends whose priorities I trust to tell me what they think I'm doing. Often I discover that I've overdone a certain point, or have been too subtle, or haven't shaded correctly with minor figures. One of the tasks of minor characters in novels, of course, is to present the development of the themes — or the counterpoint to themes — played out by the major characters. I also seek out some people I consider good general readers: people who read novels because they like to read. I want to know if they believe what I've written; if they are entertained; if they're held; if they're moved. I also seek feedback from certain writers on technical points. I also show the manuscript to my agent, to see if it's ready to sell and to get her estimate of possibilities.

Up until this time, no one will have seen the book except Ira Wood, my husband, and sometimes my oldest friend, Penny Pendleton, who's a feminist therapist in her present incarnation — she used to be a ballet dancer and a landscape architect — and with whom I worked politically for many years. I may have tried out a chapter as a magazine excerpt, or I may have read a chapter to an audience somewhere, but the novel hasn't been seen by anyone in New York.

This is partly because I don't want anyone telling me that I can't tackle a particular subject, or that something isn't commercial, or sexy, or fashionable, or whatever, before the work is essentially in place. At that point it needs some tightening, maybe some tidying, some trimming or expanding. But it stands.

Involving an editor at an earlier stage can be fatal to writing that has its own point of view. Recently I read a nonfiction book and criticized it for a flaw that the authors later told me hadn't been in the original manuscript. It was created because the male editor didn't find the women's political experiences interesting, only their personal experiences. The result was that the pain and suffering was left in but the response to it, in terms of theory and action, was stripped out, so that the women in the finished book sounded simpler, more naïve and far more passive than they actually had been.

Once a book is published it isn't mine any longer. It can't be altered or corrected by me. It belongs to you and her and him as much as to me, or more so. In fact, I feel a slight wave of embarrassment when I see it in a store window — the sort of inner blush that you undergo when you suddenly lay eyes on a lover you haven't seen in a long time: someone you shared secrets and confessions with.

A novel goes off into the world on its own, and you're lucky to get a postcard now and then — a weird review that stands the book on its head; letters from strangers full of the simmer and mud of their lives; people who call you up at three in the morning to announce that they are your heroine. Other people ignore your book and spin fantasies with it. But it's theirs now.

✳

There's a general assumption on the part of American critics and academics that anyone who writes fiction or poetry that is politically conscious must be kind of dense — that by its nature the work is cruder than work that simply embodies currently held notions; that, roughly speaking, leftist or feminist work is by definition more naïve, simpler, less profound than right-wing work. What is considered deep is writing that deals with man's fate (always *man's*) in psychospiritual terms, with our heart of darkness, somehow always darker when somebody is thinking that maybe things could be changed a little. Deep work deals with angst-filled alienation (again, always man's, because Mama has a baby and she hasn't got time for the angst). Literature is perceived, as Hans Haacke said about art, "as a mythical entity above mundane interests and ideological conflict." As Haacke also remarked, "In non-dictatorial societies, the induction into and the maintenace of a particular way of thinking and seeing must be performed with subtlety in order to succeed. Staying within the acceptable range of divergent views must be perceived as the natural thing to do." I might add that going beyond that A-to-B circuit must be perceived as unnatural, therefore discordant, strident — inherently less artistic.

As the novelist Joanna Russ has pointed out, "the expectations of the novel have narrowed to the bourgeois novel, with its preoccupation with individual success or failure." She ascribes this to a general Christian bias in favor of individual damnation or salvation, which she opposes to a more collective fiction, more profoundly Jewish, hence communal and socialist and feminist. She has defended my work in these terms, with which I'm comfortable.

I've never been able to understand the assumption that being ignorant of science is good for poets, or that being ignorant of economics and social organization is good for novelists. I've always imagined that the more curious you are about the world around you, the more you'll have to bring to your characters and to the worlds that you spin around them. I've always imagined, too, that one reason many American novelists haven't developed, but, rather, have atrophied, producing their best work out of the concerns of late adolescence and early adulthood, is that since they do not care to grapple with or even to identify the moving forces in their society they can't understand more than a few stories.

Writing that is politically conscious involves freeing the imagination, which is one reason why magic realism has been so energizing to Latin American fiction. If we view the world as static, if we think ahistorically, we lack perspective on the lives we are creating. The more variables we can link and switch in the mind, the greater our potential control over the basic and sometimes unconscious premises of our fiction and our poetry. We must be able to feel ourselves active in time and history. We choose from the infinitely complex past certain stories, certain epochs, certain struggles and battles, certain heroines and heroes that lead to us. We draw strength from them as we create our genealogy, both literarily and personally. Deciding who we are is intimately associated with who we believe our ancestors, our progenitors, our precursors are.

In the arts, particularly, we need our own sense of lineage and our own tradition to work in or to rebel against. Often we must work in a contrapuntal way to a given genre or tradition, taking it apart, slicing it against the grain, making explicit its assumptions. Think of Margaret Atwood's use of the Gothic novel tradition, or of what Joanna Russ has done to vampire stories.

A sense of false belonging destroys our ability to think and to feel. A seamless identification with a culture that excludes us as fully human or that impoverishes our options makes us limit our seeing as well as our saying. This is especially true in America, where official history is Disney World. Most of us are the grandchildren of immigrants, with parents who refused to speak whatever language was theirs as a birthright and who considered all the received history and wisdom and stories of their families as so much peasant trash to be dumped and forgotten. Often we have lost not only the names of the villages where our ancestors lived but any knowledge of what they did for a living, what they believed, why they left and came here. We have lost the history of labor and religious struggles they may have bled for. This ignorance makes us shallower than we may want to be.

A sense of political reality must not lead either to despair (the corporations are all-powerful Molochs; we cannot oppose what they do; we shall inevitably perish of nuclear war, so why bother?) or to infatuation with whatever leftist regime is currently fashionable, so that all one's efforts are spent extolling Fidel or Mao or whoever. I shall always hold in my soul as an example of the purist wrongheadedness that has often characterized the American left a devout group of comrades handing out newspapers in Central Square in Cambridge a few years ago with the banner headline FOLLOW CLOSELY COMRADE ENVER HOXHA. Central Square is a stone-working-class part of Cambridge still resisting gentrification, racially mixed and reasonably well organized along tenants' and small homeowners' lines. They have fought several successful battles against M.I.T. and for rent control. Here is an area with many problems, many energetic potential activists, and what is offered them? What sounds like a bad translation from the Albanian.

A lot of it is a case of what Indians call Wannabees — whites who want to be Indians, or what they think blacks are, or Nicaraguans, or Cubans, or Chinese, or anything at all but themselves having to figure out how to conduct a life that is useful and righteous as a live American citizen.

If we can't imagine alternative futures — new and multitudinously exciting and soothing ways to give birth, care for and socialize our young, educate each other, heal each other, marry, separate, grow old, mourn, die and be buried, communicate with fellow humans and other beings, grow food, eat, dispose of our wastes, deal with disagreements, amuse ourselves — then we shall be stuck in boredom or in the types of romanticism disguised as political doctrine that I was just mocking. We shall then want only more and more of a share of the same, or want to be those people we imagine as more real than ourselves, whether they are Chinese or living in the TV set on "Dynasty."

Imagination is powerful, whether it's working to make us envision our inner strengths and the vast en-

ergy and resources locked into ordinary people and
capable of shining out in crisis, capable of breaking
out into great good or great evil; or whether imagination is showing us utopias, dystopias or merely societies
in which some variable has changed — perhaps a society in which certain women act as incubators for the
babies of the upper echelons. When such a society is
imagined we can better understand ourselves by seeing what we are not, to better grasp what we are. We
can also then understand what we want to move toward and what we want to prevent in the worlds our
children must inhabit.

One of the hardships of being a political writer in
the United States is the mistrust of art, especially fiction, on the part of the left. There's a pervasive contempt for anything not written in leftist jargon. If it's
easy to understand, if people respond to it, it can't be
worth understanding.

A novel always seems to disturb the left because it
doesn't contain current slogans or priorities, because
it isn't true — that old Puritanical squint at fiction and
theater. It's made up. How could that be respectable?
How is that different from lying? Further, novels —
at least mine, certainly — have sex in them, too much
sex, the wrong kind of sex. The characters aren't simple enough or heroic enough to exemplify working-
class virtues.

The women's movement has been more supportive of cultural work, of creation and recreation, of the labor of hammering on the relationship between form and content, between tradition and oppression, between memory and redaction, between invention and communication. My own work has often been no less controversial in these areas, but that still doesn't excuse any of us from the necessity of art.

One strong difference between fiction and poetry is that poetry can reach people without having to depend on the New York media. Poetry readings are more important than media coverage, as is inclusion in anthologies. There are many alternative sources of information about poetry; many shades of opinion are represented in writing about it. It's very strong regionally. There's not a single source, or a few important sources, or a rating. With novels, the few reviews in New York–based publications can make or break a book in hardcover and determine whether you'll ever hear of it, whether it will be advertised, reviewed elsewhere, ordered by bookstores, or even printed a year or so later in mass paperback. The *New York Times* has tremendous power and financial clout.

Reviewers don't perceive books as having a political

dimension when the ideas expressed in the novels — who's good and who's bad, who deserves to win and what it is that's worth winning, what's considered masculine and feminine, what's normal — are congruent with the reviewers' own attitudes or with those they're used to hearing discussed over supper or at parties. When reviewers read novels whose attitudes offend them or clash with their own ideas, they perceive those novels as political and polemical, and they attack them.

Naturally I object to this system of screening books, since my novels always have something to offend everybody, but especially tend to offend the critics on the powerful periodicals. Reviewers tend to want commercial work to excite their fantasies and for literary work to conform to the standards they were taught in college, based on the work of males dead for years, whose childhoods were passed in the nineteenth century.

The mass media have also created a notion that what is packaged and consumed for use in filling hours is an escape. Doubleday used to run ads in *TV Guide* saying, "You can afford to buy more than one fantasy this month." Much popular fiction is appropriately sold in drugstores because it is in fact a drug. Many people don't read fiction anymore. If they do, they read a book the way they take an Alka-Seltzer: because they're stuck in an airport; they want to sleep; they're bored; they want some fizz. People have almost stopped expecting that fiction is going to talk to them about anything that matters in their lives.

The present structure of corporate publishing works against anyone who doesn't come from the same background, share the same problems and have the same education, the same expectations of life, the same class interests, the same sexual preferences, the same code of social right and wrong, the same sense of which emotions are fit to express publicly and which aren't permissible. It's a small world of editors. You can either write about that class for that class, or you can write fantasies of extreme sexual potency, low adventure, guns and buns, whips and whoopee. That's why, as a serious and political novelist, I urge you to support serious and political novels by buying them — and even, perhaps, by reading them.

Reviewers are not only offended if the ideas in novels affront them; they also have a notion of fiction that is centered on an individual's destiny — generally written with a great deal of introspection, graced by lively metaphors. They strongly resist fiction that takes a more collective stance, that sees each character as embedded in history and in an economic and social web. If you want examples of how such fiction is reviewed I commend to you just about every *New York Times* review of any of my novels, including the last one.

When we identify with fictional characters they offer us the opportunity to slip into someone else's skin — a woman, a man, a Black, a white, a Chicana seamstress, a Norwegian dockworker, a Japanese physicist, a politician in Kenya, a midwife in Texas, a Neanderthal woman, a sled dog, a purple arthropod from Deneb IV. When we can empathize with others we can less easily reject the alien, or what we perceive as the alien, because it truly becomes less alien to us. We imitate fictional characters. How many men still play Hemingway — a writer who played his own characters? The heroes in Byron's narrative poems inflamed a generation of young men and sometimes young women who wanted to play those parts, too. Sometimes you meet people who are still living in the late novels of Henry James, who can talk only to each other because nobody else can follow their prose.

The farther you are from the centers of power in this society, the less likely you are to find validation for your experiences, your insights, your ideas, your life. Therefore the more important it is for you to find in art that validation, that respect for your experiences that no minority except the wealthy can take for granted. Characters whom we resemble, having experiences we recognize, can help us to find a pattern in our lives. That's something we all search out in fiction. Finding a pattern in the often random and chaotic and confusing events of days and months and years is one of the functions of the novel.

How we understand our lives, the kind of choices we conceive of as possible, shapes the decisions we end up making. We all operate by myths, in part. Fiction gives us patterns by which we judge our choices, our character, our prospects. Sometimes it helps us to understand ourselves and our friends and acquaintances, as well as those whose choices are inflicted on us — people such as bosses, teachers, administrators, generals, experts and landlords. It helps us to empathize with those whom our choices and our decisions affect. We may learn that parts of ourselves that we've been taught to repress or deny are worthy of coming into daylight. We may decide that what we are ashamed of experiencing is not shameful or singular. We may see through the eyes of our parents, our children, our lovers, our supposed or real enemies, our ancestors, our descendants. We may realize what we want to happen — what kind of relationships, what kind of society we want to work toward, or work to prevent.

The conviction that those who talk differently, or look different, feel less than we do is exceedingly popular. "They don't know the value of human life in the Orient," we say, dropping bombs on them, or in Central America, or Africa, or wherever we're doing business. But one of the effects of the novel can be to induce us to identify with a character who resembles us in some way, or whom we wish we resembled, even if in ordinary life we wouldn't recognize that resemblance because the externals are so dissimilar. The novelist may even seduce the reader into identifying with characters whom he or she would refuse to know in ordinary life. Very few people who read my novel *Woman on the Edge of Time* would have anything to do with the protagonist — a middle-aged, overweight Chicana defined as crazy, shabbily dressed, lucky to get off welfare and into a mopwoman's job.

I consider fiction one way of persuading people to cross those borders of alienation and mistrust into the existence of someone in whose mind and body a reader may find it enlightening to spend some time. Fiction works no miracles of conversion, but I guess I do believe that any white reader who spends a reasonable amount of time consuming Black novels and Black poetry is less likely to be as comfortably racist in large and small ways, and that any man who reads enough of current women's literature is less likely to be ignorant of what women want and need and don't want and don't need.

Some experiences that become incorporated in fiction into one or another character, or that are used in poems, are of that sturdy, common, shared sort that you have confidence will touch many readers. But some experienced or imagined material will cause you to feel shame and trepidation, especially if you are a woman. You'll fear on the one hand that you are exposing too much of yourself and that you'll go around naked to the world afterward. This is perhaps even more true of poetry than of fiction, where it's always possible to disown a character — to say, "That was a crazy woman, of course. That's how crazy people behave." In poetry, unless you're writing with a carefully created persona, people tend to assume that even poems created totally of other people's experiences are autobiographical and to attribute everything directly to you.

You're afraid on the other hand that people will say, "That's ridiculous. Nobody acts that way (except you). No woman feels that way toward her child/husband/lover/mother." You have to have a commitment to the truths wrung from yourself as well as to the truths already made public from our common history. It is not less important when you are writing with a more collective or historical sense than when you are writing more narrowly.

For women, many of our experiences were dumb to us — unnamed, unpossessed because misnamed. I had insights at fifteen that I would seize again at twenty-six and lose again, because I had no intellectual or imaginative framework in which they might fit and be retained. As writers we are always asking in public, through our work, whether our experiences and those of other people with whom we empathize and from whom we create are experiences common to at least part of the population, or whether the experiences we are working with are crazy, singular and bizarre. There are inner censors who make shallow or imitative or tentative or coy the work of a writer, often through fear.

Voices speak in our heads, telling us that we are brazen to admit certain things, that we should be ashamed. We may fear to offend those with power over us, or to hurt those whom we wish to love us or whom we wish to please. We may fear that those whose politics we share and whose good opinions we rely on may dislike work that deals with the contradictions between ideology and action. Yet such contradictions are rich to writers. Often we grasp our characters most firmly in those moist, irrational interstices between intention and delivery, between rhetoric and greed, between image and fear.

As women we have been trained to deny our anger, and when it emerges in a poem we are often ashamed. Poems are never complete statements. In one day you can write two equally truthful poems — one, of the most intense, overwhelming love for a person, the other of equally intense and complete hostility for the same person. You may write an extremely moving love poem addressed to no one in particular, but to a fusion of people.

Shame can get in creation's way. We all have notions of what we should be. A writer had better have considerable tolerance for that gap between what we'd like to be and what we are in our daily lives. At the same time, it helps a writer to have experience about how extraordinary people can be in situations that stretch them utterly. Sometimes we're ashamed of what moves us, or of how much we're moved. At other times we feel that we ought to have been moved and we try to pretend. We don't only fake orgasms; people have faked orgiastic appreciation of many things that bored and even affronted them, from the Grand Canyon to their party's heroes and rhetoric.

As a poet and as a novelist I have to believe that when I go into myself honestly, to use what I find there, it's going to speak to you. Some of our experiences — yours and mine — are similar and some are different, but the naming of both liberates us. Using the feelings that may be different seems more dangerous to me, as I may stand alone in giving them voice, yet I think these experiences too are extremely important for us.

Writing politically, writing as a feminist, writing as a serious woman, doesn't mean writing comic books and calling them novels. It doesn't mean creating impossible, good, heroic, pure, strong, healthy, no-fault, no-ulcers women who run around in seven-league boots, righting wrongs before breakfast. Writers aren't in the business of fulfilling anyone's fantasies, even those of the oppressed. The oppressed sometimes indulge in their own fantasies of power. As a child I really wanted magic; only magic would make me able to push around those who were bigger and stronger than I was. We still want magic, sometimes to right the balance.

But don't ask real novelists, in real novels, to write wish-fulfillment fantasies, for all such books are soft to the core. They evaporate and leave nothing, as a Popsicle does when it melts. Our writers must tell us stories and create us characters that have more truth in them than wishes — stories that have enough grit and power to wound as well as to please. As readers we have to be willing to be made sad when we confront art, to let it hurt us, move us, shake us, make us dissatisfied and then satisfy us with vision, with passion, with contemplation, with the perception of form, of pattern. Patterns in the universe are not designed to comfort us. The spiral nebula may be beautiful, but it doesn't make us feel any more secure or more self-important. We have to be willing to be set on edge.

In a stratified society all literature is engaged politically and morally, whether it's so perceived by the author or not. It will be so perceived by the readers it validates and by the readers it affronts. This doesn't mean that I think a novel or a poem can be judged by some utilitarian criterion. Art is only partly rational. It acts on all the levels of our brain and influences us through sounds and silences, through identification and imagery, through rhythms and chemistry.

But as writers and readers, the literature we read makes us more or less sensitive to each other. Poems and novels tell us how we may expect to experience love and hatred, violence and peace, birth and death. They deeply influence what we expect to find as our love object, and what we expect to enjoy on the job or in bed, and what we think is okay for others to enjoy. They help us decide what war is like — a boring hell or a necessary masculine maturation experience in a jolly peer group — and therefore whether we are willing to be drafted to fight one. They cause us to expect that rape is a shattering experience of violence, like being struck by a hit-and-run truck, or a titillating escapade that all women secretly desire. They influence our daydreams and our fantasies and therefore what we believe other people offer us or are withholding from us.

I think it's healthy for us to remember where the impulses to say poems and to tell stories come from. Our work should touch those centers of the psyche from which the urge to make and receive it come. Art doesn't progress the way physics progresses. In art we don't build better bombs. We don't know more about poetry than Sappho did, or tell a better story than Homer did. It's new. It's new always. It's made again. Like love. Like anger.

For me, writing fiction issues from the impulse to tell the story of people who deserve to have their lives examined and their stories told, to people who deserve to read good stories. I'm responsible to many people with buried lives: people who have been rendered as invisible in history as they are powerless in the society their work creates, populates, cleans, repairs and defends. For me the impulse to write poems comes from the desire to give permanent voice to something in the experience of a life. To find ourselves spoken for in art gives dignity to our pain, our anger, our lust, our losses. We can hear what we hope for, and what we most fear, in the small release of cadenced utterances. We have few rituals that function as well for us in the ordinary chaos of our lives as art can. The pattern, imposed perhaps but nonetheless satisfying, emerges from the utterance, from the story. It's made new again if we're clear-hearted and work hard, and that's enough miracle for me.

———

Q. In addition to reading and writing, how are you politically involved?

A. I've been politically active my whole life. Nobody can tell you what issues to work on. You work on the issues that move you. It all has to be done. As long as you do something to move it forward it doesn't really matter which issues you pick out, or whether other people like them or not.

Q. Where do you find the time?

A. I don't put as much time into political activism as I did when I was younger. When I was younger I did that at least half the time. Realistically, I reach a lot more people now with my writing than I do with political organizing, so I don't do as much political organizing and I do it in a different way. It's just a question of payoff of time and impact. But how do I find the time? I take the time. Basically, I get up early. If you get up early and get your own writing done early enough you do the other things afterward. There's very little politically that people ever want you to do at six in the morning. When I was a full-time political activist the only way I got any writing done was by getting up earlier than anybody else in the New York movement.

Q. Who influenced you before you started writing? Who were the most influential poets and the most influential novelists?

A. Well, you're going back to age fifteen — a working-class girl in Detroit at fifteen, I was influenced by Emily Dickinson and Walt Whitman. What was I reading then? Probably Freud and Marx and *The Golden Bough*. There were two examples that moved me a whole lot when I was that age — about college age. One was Muriel Rukeyser as a poet. She seemed so strong and so female and so political and so intelligent and so together. She wasn't getting much for it, but she was just such a fantastic poet. She moved me a great deal. And the example of Simone de Beauvoir was terribly important. Here was someone who was writing both politically and personally and who seemed to be trying to do all kinds of interesting things. I was very excited by her and very moved by her. She's probably the closest thing to a crush heroine I ever had.

GORE VIDAL

The Agreed-Upon Facts

SOME MONTHS AGO *Newsweek* asked me to write a page on Ollie North and the Iran-contra Senate hearings. In the course of my remarks I not only betrayed a lack of sympathy for Ollie, but I was unkind about the President who had wound him up and set him loose and then forgotten all about him. Well, on the page opposite me in the magazine was an endorsement of Ollie and Ron by Pat Buchanan. A few days after this inflammatory issue of *Newsweek* appeared I got a call from *Time* magazine's White House correspondent, Hugh Sidey, who has been covering the presidency ever since Mr. Lincoln's death. During that time Hugh has never met a President he couldn't worship.

So Hugh said, "Hi, Gore," and I said, "Hi, Hugh" — we're big on first names inside the Beltway. Hugh said, "I was with the President and Nancy at Camp David over the weekend, and he read your *Newsweek* piece."

"What did he think, Hugh?" I asked.

But Hugh was too foxy for me. He said, "The President said, with a twinkle in his eye, 'Vidal always gets things wrong. Why, he has a scene in *Lincoln* where he has Lincoln looking out his office window at the sunrise. And you can't see the sun rise from the office.' Is there, Gore, such a scene in your book? My researcher here at *Time* can't find it."

"No, Hugh," I said, "there is no such scene, as Mr. Lincoln didn't get up as early as Mr. Reagan."

"Oh," said Hugh. In the next issue of *Time* Hugh Sidey quoted President Reagan as saying that Gore Vidal is inaccurate because he has Lincoln seeing something from the White House that *he* couldn't see.

Now this is what we historians call, excitedly, a "primary source" and what journalists call "investigative journalism." Later I figured out that Ron thought Lincoln's office was the Oval Office, but that wasn't built until 1904. Later still I realized that I had been attacked at some length by folks who love Reagan and don't love me, and that Pat Buchanan had probably repeated to Ron one of their accusations. Ron, although his nose is never out of a book, hasn't, I think, really read *Lincoln*, unlike Mondale, who, after his first triumphant debate with Reagan on television, told the press he was taking the weekend off to read *Lincoln*, which he did, and lost the election. Attach whatever moral to that you like.

This evening I'm going to answer, very briefly, those critics who gave Pat the ammunition for Ron to discredit my accuracy because I had criticized Ollie in *Newsweek*.

In the beginning there was the spoken word. The first narrations concerned the doings of gods and kings, and these stories were passed on from generation to generation, usually as verse in order to make memorizing easier. Then, mysteriously, in the fifth century B.C., all the narratives were written down, and literature began. But from Greece to Persia to India to China there was a great controversy: Could a narrative be possessed that had been committed to writing rather than to memory? Traditionalists said no, modernists said yes. The traditionalists lost. Now, twenty-five hundred years later, there is a similar crisis. Modernists believe that any form of narration and of learning can be transmitted through audio-visual means rather than through the now-traditional written word. In this controversy I am, for once, a conservative to the point of furious reaction. In any case, we are now obliged to ask radical questions: What is the point in writing things down, other than to give directions on how to operate a machine? Why tell stories about gods and kings, or even about men and women?

Very early, the idea of fame — eternal fame — afflicted our race. But fame for the individual was less intense at the beginning than fame for one's tribe. Thucydides is often read as a sort of biographer of Pericles, when indeed he was writing the biography (to misuse the word) of their city, Athens. It is the idea of the city that the writer wants us to understand, not the domestic affairs of Pericles, which he mentions only as civic illustrations. Love, as opposed to lust, hadn't yet been discovered, and marriage wasn't yet a subject, except for comedy; Sophocles didn't care who got custody of the children unless Medea killed them or they were baked in a pie.

For more than two millennia, from Homer to Aeschylus to Dante to Shakespeare to Tolstoy, the great line of our literature has concerned itself with gods, heroes and kings in conflict with one another and with inexorable fate. Simultaneously, all around each story, whether it be that of Prometheus or some Plantagenet prince, there is a people who need fire from heaven or land beyond the sea. "Of arms and of the man I sing" means just that: of the people then and now, of the hero then and his image now, as created or recreated by the poet. From the beginning the bard, the poet, the writer, was a most high priest to his people, the custodian of their common memory, the interpreter of their history, the voice of their current yearnings.

All this stopped in the last two centuries, when the rulers decided to teach the workers to read and write so that they could handle machinery. Traditionalists thought this was a dangerous experiment. If the common people knew too much, might they not overthrow their masters? But the modernists, like John Stuart Mill, won. And in due course the people, proudly literate, overthrew their masters. We got rid of the English, while the French and the Russians — ardent readers — shredded their ancient monarchies. In fact, the French, who read and theorize more than any other people, became so addicted to political experiment that in the two centuries since our own rather drab revolution they have exuberantly produced one Directory, one Consulate, two empires, three restorations of the monarchy and five republics. That's what happens when you take writing too seriously. Happily, Americans have never liked reading all that much. Politically ignorant, we keep sputtering along in our old Model T, looking wistfully every four years for a good mechanic.

Along with political change — the result of general literacy and the printing press — the nature of narrative began to fragment. High literature concerned itself, most democratically, with the doings of common folk. Although a George Eliot or a Hardy could make art out of these simple domestic tales, in most hands crude mirrors of life tend to be duller than Dumas, say, and, paradoxically, less popular. Today's serious novel is apt to be a carefully written, teacherly text about people who teach school and write teacherly texts to dwindling classes. Today's popular novel, carelessly, recklessly composed on — or sometimes by — a machine, paradoxically has taken over the heroes and kings and gods, placing them in modern designer clothes among consumer dreams beyond the dreams of Scheherazade.

This is a very strange reversal. The best writers tend to write, in a highly minimal way, of the simple and the dull, while the worst writers give us whirlwind tours of the House — I'm sorry, the home — of

Atreus, ripping every skeleton from its closet and throwing back every Porthault sheet. The fact that this kind of bad writing is popular isn't because the reading public — an endangered minority — cherishes bad writing for its own sake but because the good writers fail to interest them. As a result, everything is now so totally out of whack that the high academic bureaucrats have dropped literature, with some relief, and replaced it with literary theory — something that one needs no talent to whip up. During the last twenty years enrollment in college English departments has fallen by almost 60 percent. Writers and writing no longer matter very much anywhere in freedom's land. Mistuh Emerson, he dead. Our writers are just entertainers, and aren't that entertaining, either. We have lost the traditional explainer, examiner, prophet.

So what am I doing here? If nothing else, I continue endlessly to explain, to examine, to prophesy, particularly in those five novels where I deal with the history of the United States from the beginning to now. The fact that there is still a public interested in finding out who we are and what we did ought to encourage other writers to join me. But, by and large, universities have made that impossible. They have established a hegemony over every aspect of literature except the ability to make any. They have also come to believe that a serious novelist deals only with what he knows, and since our educational system is what it is, he's not apt to know much about anything, and since our class system is uncommonly rigid he's not going to have much chance to find out about any world other than the one he was born into — and the school he later went to. Certainly he will never, like his predecessors, be able to deal with the nation's rulers. (They prefer the shadows, in any case.) Mary McCarthy recently listed all the things you can't put into a serious novel today, from a sunset to a hanging to a Cabinet meeting. Also, to be fair, though our political life is entirely devoid of politics, it's so vivid with personalities and the stuff of bad fiction that one can hardly expect the novelist to compete with the journalist. Or with Ted Koppel.

One of the absolutes of book-chat land is that the historical novel is neither history nor a novel. On the other hand, a literate record of a contemporary murder is by definition, triumphantly, a novel. This is what I call "the Capote confusion." His monument. Actually there's no such thing as "The Novel," as opposed to Novels. No one can say what a novel ought to be. History is something else. Although I try to make the agreed-upon facts as accurate as possible, I always use the phrase "agreed-upon" because what we know of a figure as recent as, let's say, Theodore Roosevelt is not only not the whole truth — an impossibility anyway — but the so-called facts are often contradicted by other facts.

So one must select, and it's in selection that literature begins. To start with, *whose* facts do you agree with? Also, in a novel, as opposed to a literal history, one can introduce made-up characters who can speculate on the motives of the real people. How real are the real people? Do I have them say what they really said, or am I, like Shakespeare, reinventing them? For those of you ablaze with curiosity regarding the difference between Shakespeare and me, I'll give you an example.

There is in Washington, D.C., my native city and often subject, a South Korean newspaper called the *Washington Times*. This paper is owned by the Moonies and its political line is baroquely neo-Fascist. Now I'll show you one of their employees in action. The first scene of a recent book of mine, *Empire*, takes place in England at a country house that has been rented for the summer of 1898 by Henry Adams and Senator Don Cameron for the use of their friend John Hay, the American ambassador to England. All those present at a lunch that I describe were actually there, including Henry James, an old friend of Hay and of Adams, who is living in nearby Rye.

Confronted with such a scene, the hostile reviewer, who writes only of what he knows, often shouts "name-dropper." But how is it possible to tell the story of John Hay without mentioning that, say, as Lincoln's secretary, he did get to meet Lincoln? The South Korean reviewer does the ritual attack on me. I hate my native land because I deplore the current administration. Because I deplore our imperial adventures I am an isolationist. And he goes on to say: "Henry James and Henry Adams figure in *Empire*, neither of them believably, alas . . . for their main function is to serve as spokesmen for Mr. Vidal's isolationism. 'You speak of the laws of history and I am no lawyer,' says the Vidalized James. 'But I confess to misgivings. How can we, who honestly cannot govern ourselves, take up the task of governing others? Are we to govern the Philippines from Tammany Hall?' " Now the reviewer says, "Neither in style nor in substance does this mini-editorial sound even remotely like Henry James." That's pretty strong stuff. Plainly a James scholar.

Now let's look at what Henry James actually wrote apropos the Spanish-American War. In a letter he remarks on his "deep embarrassment of thought — of imagination. I have hated, I have almost loathed this war." James also speaks most sardonically of the exportation of Tammany and King Caucus to the newly acquired Philippines: "remote countries run by bosses." My South Korean critic didn't quote what is easily the harshest of the Vidalized Henry James remarks: "The acquisition of an empire civilized the English. That may not be a law but it is a fact. . . . But what civilized them might very well demoralize us even further." That's about as anti-imperial — or isolationist — as you can get. Did the real Henry James ever say so un-American a thing? Yes, he did, when he confided to his nephew Harry: "Expansion has so made the English what they are — for good or for ill, but on the whole for good — that one doesn't quite feel one's way to say for one's country, 'No — I'll have none of it.' Empire has educated the English. Will it only demoralize us?"

Now you see how I have had James say, in substance, precisely what he did say. I do condense — something a biographer must never do, but which a novelist must do. If my James is not credible, then he himself would not be credible to a jingo on a Washington newspaper, who also tells us that my invented Caroline could never have taken over a Washington newspaper and made a success of it. But less than twenty years later my old friend Eleanor Patterson did exactly that. As for America's perennially venal press, the *Washington Times* reviewer would be stunned to hear Henry James in real life blame the newspapers for the despicable war with Spain, because of "the horrible way in which they envenomize all dangers and reverberate all lies." Like Mark Twain and William Dean Howells, James was, incredibly, an isolationist with a contempt for the popular press. So as you can see, I don't invent my literary ancestors. If anything, they invented me.

I have mentioned "agreed-upon facts" as the stuff of history. But if it's impossible to take seriously the press of one's own time, even Hugh Sidey, why should the historian treat old newspapers as unimpeachable primary sources? For instance, I'm now writing about Warren Harding. One of the few quotations of Harding that I've known all my life was what he said after his unlikely nomination for the presidency: "We drew to a pair of deuces, and filled." This poker reference (for you card players) strikes absolutely the right note for the agreed-upon Harding that our canting society requires: a sleazy, poker-playing, hard-drinking, womanizing nonentity, put in office by cynical Republican bosses. Yet the journalist Mark Sullivan was with Harding before, during and after the 1920 convention. In his book *Our Times* he quotes the poker phrase; then, in a footnote, he says that this sort of phrase was not characteristic of Harding, who had a considerable sense of his own dignity. Apparently Sullivan, who could have asked Harding at any time during the next three years whether he had made this remark, never did. Instead he tells us that maybe Harding said it when he was "off-balance" from excitement. "Or he may never have said it — it may have been some reporter's conception of what he ought to say."

There we have it. In effect, the press invents us all. And the later biographer or historian can only select, from the mass of crude fictions and part-truths, those "facts" that his contemporaries are willing to agree upon.

Where many English departments now favor literary theory over literature, the history departments — too often drudging bureaucracies — are solemnly aware that their agreed-upon facts must constitute, at least in the short term, a view of the Republic that will please the university's trustees. Since all great Americans are uniquely great, even saints, those who regard the lives of these saints are hagiographers. This is quite a big, solemn business, not unlike the bureaucracy of some huge advertising firm handling a hallowed account like Ivory soap. One major bureaucrat today is C. Vann Woodward, Sterling Professor of History Emeritus at Yale. A Southerner, he noticed many years ago that blacks were people. This Newtonian revelation brought him tenure and landed him many important accounts. Like most academic bureaucrats, the Sterling Professor is highly protective of his turf; he doesn't want the untenured loose in his field. Sadly, he noted in the pages of the *New York Review of Books*, regarding my *Lincoln*, that "the book was extravagantly praised by both novelists and historians — a few of the latter at least. Some of the foremost Lincoln scholars do not share these views. After listing numerous historical blunders and errors in the novel, Richard N. Current, a leading Lincoln biographer, declares that 'Vidal is wrong on big as well as little matters. He grossly distorts Lincoln's character and role in history.'"

Woodward gives no examples of these distortions. He does tell us that "Roy P. Basler, editor of *The Collected Works of Abraham Lincoln*, estimates that 'more than half of the book could never have happened as told by Vidal.'" Apparently Woodward believes that it's sufficient merely to assert. He does not demonstrate, doubtless because he is innocent of the text in question. So he cites, vaguely, other assertions. As it turns out, his two authorities inspired our President, indirectly, to the higher criticism. Hence I bring up my own defense here.

Vladimir Nabokov said that when anyone criticized his art he was indifferent — that was their problem. But if anyone attacked his scholarship he reached for his dictionary. After reading Woodward I took the trouble to read the two very curious little essays that he cites. What case do they make? Is half the book all wrong? And is Lincoln himself greatly distorted? Although I do my own research, unlike so many professors, whose hagiographies are usually the work of these indentured servants the graduate students, when it comes to checking a finished manuscript I turn to Academe — here, in the case of *Lincoln,* to Professor David H. Donald of Harvard, who has written a great deal about the period, which the Sterling Professor, as far as I recall, hasn't written about at all. I also use a professional researcher to correct dates, names and agreed-upon facts.

In his critique of my book Professor Current fusses, not irrelevantly, about the fictionalizing of actual political figures. I also fuss about this. But he has fallen prey to the scholar-squirrels' delusion that there is a final Truth, revealed only to the tenured in their footnote maze. In this he is simply naïve. All we have is a mass of more or less agreed-upon facts about the illustrious dead, and each generation tends to rearrange those facts according to what the times require. Current's text seethes with resentment, and I can see why. He says, "Indeed, Vidal claims to be a better historian than any of the academic writers on Lincoln." Current's source for my unseemly boasting is, God help us, the Larry King radio show, which lasts several hours from midnight on and you're not under oath on anything you say after twelve o'clock at night. On the other hand, I must confess that Larry King as a source is about as primary as you can get.

Actually, he misheard me. It's true that I have been amazed that there has never been a first-rate biography of Lincoln, as opposed to many very good and highly scholarly studies of various aspects of his career. One reason for this lack is that the bureaucrats of Academe have largely taken over the writing of history, and most of them neither write well nor, worse, understand the nature of the men they are required to make saints of. In the past, history was the province of literary masters — of Gibbon, of Macaulay, of Burke, of Locke, of Carlyle — and, in our time, of Academe's *bête noir*, Edmund Wilson. In principle, it would be better if English teachers didn't write novels and history teachers didn't write history. After all, teaching itself is a great and essential profession — marvelously ill-practiced in our country, as was recently demonstrated when half of today's college freshmen couldn't locate, on an unmarked map of the world, the United States.

By and large, Current's complaints range from the trivial to the pointless. Does he find me wrong on anything of consequence? Yes, he does. And I think it the whole point to his weird enterprise. Current tells us that "there is no convincing evidence" for Vidal's contention that "as late as April 1865, Lincoln was still planning to colonize freed slaves outside the United States." This is a delicate point in the 1980s, when no national saint can be suspected of racism.

I turned to one of my authorities for this statement, and I realized that I may have relied on suspect scholarship. Here's the passage I used: "Lincoln to the last seemed to have a lingering preference for another kind of amendment, another kind of plan. He still clung to his old ideas of postponing final emancipation, compensating slave holders, and colonizing freedmen. Or so it would appear. As late as March of 1865, if the somewhat dubious Ben Butler is to be believed, Lincoln summoned him to the White House to discuss with him the feasibility of removing the colored population of the United States."

That passage is from a book called *The Lincoln Nobody Knows* by Richard N. Current.

So either Current is as wrong about this as he is about me, or he is right, and between March and that April day, when Lincoln departed this vale of tears, the President changed his mind on the colonizing of slaves. If he did, there's no record known to me — or, I suspect, to anyone.

What is going on here is a deliberate revision, by Current and others, not only of Lincoln but of himself in order to serve the saint in the 1980s, as opposed to the saint at earlier times, when blacks were still colored, having only just stopped being Negroes. In colored and Negro days the saint would have wanted them out of the country, as Lincoln did. But in the age of Martin Luther King, Jr., even the most covertly racist of school boards must agree that a saint like Abraham Lincoln could never have wanted a single black person to leave freedom's land, much less bravery's home. So all the hagiographers are redoing their plaster images, and anyone who draws attention to the discrepancy between their own past crudities and their present attitudes is a very bad person indeed.

Woodward's other authority, Roy P. Basler, writes rather the way W. C. Fields's Southern foil, Grady

Sutton, acted. Fields once turned to Sutton and said,
"The trouble with you, my boy, is that you have too
much of the tomboy in you." Well, there's a lot of
tomboy in Basler. He is given to frantic Grady Sutton
hyperbole. He declares Carl Sandburg's multivolume
biography of Lincoln a "monumental achievement,"
which should have been a warning to me. It's a monument all right — to a plaster saint of the kind that
these two professional hagiographers are paid to keep
dusted. Basler finds my *Lincoln* "the phoniest historical novel I have ever had the pleasure of reading."
Also, he says, "More than half the book could never
have happened as told." Unfortunately, he doesn't say
which half. If I knew, we could cut the phony half
from the good half and publish the result as Basler's
Vidal's Lincoln.

Like Current, Basler gets all tangled up in misread
or misunderstood trivia. He is also most protective of
the saint. For instance, every saint is a kind and indul-
gent yet gently stern father, devoted to his children,
who worship him. But Lincoln's oldest son, Robert,
didn't like his father. Basler gets all trembly as he
writes, "When Vidal has Robert Lincoln say to Hay
about his father, 'He hates his past. He hates having
been a scrub . . . he wanted me to be what he
couldn't be,' I find no excuse. Robert did admit that

he and his father had never been close after he was grown, and he may have felt neglected, but for him to speak thus is beyond comprehension."

But he did speak thus — to Senator Thomas Pryor Gore of Oklahoma, my grandfather, who often talked to me about Robert's bleak attitude toward his father and how, having sent his son to Exeter and Harvard in order to move him up in the world, Lincoln found that he had a son with whom he didn't have much in common. I myself attended Exeter, four score years after Robert, and memories of Lincoln were still vivid, and well described not long ago in the alumni bulletin: how Lincoln spoke at the chapel and enthralled the boys and delighted everyone and ignored his son.

Basler, like Current, is eager to bring the saint into the mainstream of today's political mythology. Both are appalled whenever I mention Lincoln's scheme for colonizing the ex-slaves. Both deny that he ever had anything but love and admiration for blacks and considered them in every way his equals once slavery was past. "The one thing I most resented," writes Basler, "is the perpetuation of 'Lincoln's unshaken belief that the colored race was inferior to the white. . . .' I have never found any such categorical avowal in anything Lincoln wrote or was reported to have said." Yet Basler himself wrote in *The Lincoln Legend*,

"[Lincoln] never contemplated with any degree of satisfaction the prospect of a free Negro race living in the same country with a free white race." Not even I have dared go so far as to suggest that, as a novelist, I've ever had any way of knowing what Lincoln may or may not have *contemplated!* Basler, like Current, is revising himself.

Actually, Lincoln's views of blacks were common to his time and place, but, as he was an uncommon man, he tried to transcend them, as he did in a speech in Peoria in 1854. "My first impulse," he said rather daringly for that year, "would be to free all slaves and send them to Liberia." He then lists all the objections that others would later make to him. He finally throws in the towel when he asks: "Free them and make them politically and socially our equals? Our own feelings must not admit of it, and if mine would, we well know that those of the great mass of whites will not."

So there it is — what this little polemic is all about. As you can see, it is my radical view that Americans are now sufficiently mature to be shown a Lincoln as close to the original as it's possible for us so much later in time to render. As I too am a saint, not yet plaster — or even plastered — I sympathize with the Currents and the Baslers and with anyone else who teaches school or, to be precise, takes a teacher's salary from a History Department because he must keep all the saints up-to-date or perish. Nevertheless, since the tragic race war goes on as fiercely as ever in this country — a famous battleground is only half a block from this room — I think candor about blacks and whites and racism is more than ever necessary. It was part of Lincoln's greatness that unlike those absolute abolitionists, the radical Republicans, he foresaw the long, ugly confrontation and tried to spare future generations by geographically separating the races. The fact that his plan was not only impractical but inadvertently cruel is beside the point. He wanted to *do* something. And he never let go of the subject, unless of course he had a vision in the last two weeks of his life, known only to Mr. Current.

So how do I do what I do? And why?

I assemble what is known, and I'm grateful, as always, to actual scholars, as opposed to hagiographers. Then I start to look for a pattern or an image. And in this I am the reverse of the usual academic bureaucrat. I never know where I'll end or what I'll find along the way. If I did, such labor would be unbearable and pointless.

What did I find about Lincoln that I didn't know? The excellent Herbert Mitgang, an amateur Lincoln scholar like me, took me to task indirectly when he wrote not long ago: "Several revisionist academics have advanced the incredible theory that Lincoln really wanted the Civil War, with its 600,000 casualties, in order to eclipse the Founding Fathers and insure his own place in the pantheon of great presidents." Well, there's no single motive driving anyone, but, yes, that's pretty much what I came to believe as Lincoln himself got more and more mystical about the Union, and less and less logical in his defense of it, and more and more appalled at all the blood and at those changes in his country which, he confessed — with pride? — were "fundamental and astounding."

If Lincoln had followed Secretary of State Seward's line he could have let the Southern states go, and then in time taken them back, as they had no place to go. But great men are in almost no way like others — something that's hard for schoolteachers, perhaps, to grasp. All through the passion play of Lincoln's presidency I could hear his own words, spoken at the age of twenty-nine, reverberate in my head. In a speech at Springfield he praised the Founding Fathers and their Republic. Then he went on:

This field of glory is harvested, and the crop is already appropriated. But new reapers will arise, and they too will seek a field. It is to deny what the history of the world tells us is true to suppose that men of ambitions and talents will not continue to spring up amongst us. And when they do, they will as naturally seek the gratification of their ruling passions as others have done before them. The question, then, is can that gratification be found in supporting and maintaining an edifice that has been erected by others? Most certainly it cannot.

Thus Lincoln warns us against Lincoln. And he goes on:

Towering genius disdains a beaten path. It seeks regions unexplored. . . . It denies that it is glory enough to serve under any chief. It scorns to tread in the path of any predecessor however illustrious. It thirsts and burns for distinction; and, if possible, it will have it, whether at the expense of emancipating slaves or enslaving free men.

Nothing that Shakespeare ever invented was to equal Lincoln's invention of himself — and, in the process, us. What the Trojan War was to the Greeks, the Civil War is to us. What the wily Ulysses was to the Greeks, the wily Lincoln is to us — not plaster saint but towering genius, our haunted and haunting re-creator.

Q. I once heard a quote attributed to Lincoln: "I shall study to prepare myself, and my opportunity must come." Did that ever come up in your research?

A. I came across things like that about Lincoln's ambition, particularly in Herndon, his law partner, who knew him best. He said that Lincoln's ambition was like a little clock going tick-tick-tick. It never stopped.

Q. *Do you like Lincoln the man?*

A. Well, he's irresistible as a person. He's formidaable. He's terribly funny. I'm always asked the question Could Lincoln run for office today in the age of television? because he wasn't very handsome, and so on. For God's sake, he was the greatest stand-up comic of his time. He could take over the Johnny Carson show and do the monologue every night. Better! He was one of the wittiest men who ever lived. When he went out on the circuit as a lawyer in Illinois, every time he came to town the entire court would gather round for Lincoln to start improvising, and he would go from story to story and he'd have them hysterical.

Do I like Lincoln the titan? No, he gives me the willies — I don't ever want to see one of those again. The Civil War didn't need to take place. He could have stopped it, and he didn't. I believe very much that speech I quoted at the end — that he didn't want to be the heir of Washington; he wanted to be Lincoln and to begin a new country. Why is he always talking about "this house" and "rededicating" and "starting over again"? He gives himself away. That Lincoln I don't like. The man you couldn't help but admire.

Another fascinating thing about him to me, is: How on earth did a man who had only about two years of formal education — in fact, it was hardly education — turn out to have the best prose style of almost any American except Ulysses S. Grant, who went to West Point — which doesn't have a good English Department? How did these two men suddenly write such extraordinary prose: Grant's memoirs and Lincoln's speeches? Where did that come from? Lincoln never read novels and he never read biographies. He read a lot of poetry, generally bad, and he read and reread Shakespeare. His favorite play was *Macbeth*. There are clues from *Macbeth* all over the place, while "Oh, my offense is rank" (*Hamlet*) was one of his great numbers. Part of the greatness was that Lincoln himself was far from certain that he had done the right thing.

Bibliography

When we were planning this series of talks it occurred to us that we would like to know what books these writers remembered or found helpful, influential or inspirational in writing their own political novels. This informal bibliography is their answer to our request.

ROBERT STONE

The following might be said to be the core of my formative reading: Dickens's *Pickwick Papers* and *Great Expectations*; Saroyan's *Human Comedy*; *Look Homeward, Angel* by Thomas Wolfe; Hemingway's *Sun Also Rises* and *Hills Like White Elephants*;

Steinbeck's *Cannery Row;* Dos Passos's *USA; The Return of the Native* by Thomas Hardy; Kafka's *Trial;* Joyce's *Dubliners* and *A Portrait of the Artist as a Young Man;* Conrad's *Victory;* Malraux's *Man's Fate.*

Carlyle's *History of the French Revolution;* St. Augustine's *Confessions;* Engels's *History of the Peasant War in Germany; The Pursuit of the Millennium* by Norman Cohn; Chesterton's *Life of Dickens; Wild Life Under the Equator* by Paul du Chaillu; *The Parable of the Beast* by John Bleibtreu.

ISABEL ALLENDE

I have always been a very disorganized reader. I think that the greatest influences on my writing are the books that I read when I was a child — books that gave me the love of adventure and risk, strong characters and rich plots.

The favorite writers of my childhood were Emilio Salgari, Mark Twain, Shakespeare, Tolstoy, Henri Troyat, Chekhov.

I remember two great books of adventure — *A Thousand and One Nights* and the Bible, which I read with a total lack of religious inclination.

I suppose that in my adult life I have been influenced by others, like Pablo Neruda, García Márquez, Alejo Carpentier and the North American feminists I read in the early seventies.

Some movies have also left a great mark in my imagination, and I owe most of my inspiration to the oral tradition of storytelling of the women in my family.

CHARLES McCARRY

Because political conviction is akin to religious faith, the following basic texts are good friends to the writer of fiction who wishes to show the believer in action:

The Revised Standard Version of the Bible and the King James Bible, read in conjunction with each other; Ignatius Loyola's *Spiritual Exercises;* Darwin's *Origin of Species;* Marx's *Capital;* the correspondence of Sigmund Freud; Jung's *Memory, Dreams, and Reflections;* J. G. Frazer's *The Golden Bough;* and the scholarship and anecdotage — and especially the correspondence — connected to these works and their authors.

Also: Herodotus; Plutarch's *Lives;* Suetonius's

Lives of the Caesars; Malory's *Morte D'Arthur;* Jacob Burckhardt's *Civilization of the Renaissance in Italy;* Machiavelli's *Prince; The Diary of Samuel Pepys,* for the accounts of his relations with his royal and noble patrons and his work as clerk of the Admiralty; *England Under the Stuarts* by G. M. Trevelyan; Lord Macaulay's *History of England; The Life and Death of Adolf Hitler* by Robert Payne; *Inside the Third Reich* by Albert Speer; *Benito Mussolini* by Christopher Hibbert; the memoirs of Charles de Gaulle; *Quotations from Chairman Mao Tse-tung.*

Candide; Henry IV, Part II; Huckleberry Finn; Sandburg's *Lincoln;* Gertrude Stein's commentary on the politics of friendship, *The Autobiography of Alice B. Toklas;* Malraux's *Man's Fate;* Robert Graves's Claudius novels; George Orwell's books of reportage, especially *Down and Out in Paris and London* and *Homage to Catalonia;* Joyce Cary's *Mister Johnson* (and all the rest of his books); Evelyn Waugh's war trilogy and *Waugh in Abyssinia;* Alexander Solzhenitsyn's *Gulag Archipelago* and *The Third Circle;* Graves's *Goodbye to All That;* André Schwarz-Bart's *The Last of the Just;* W. Somerset Maugham's *Writer's Notebook,* for the account of his secret mission to Russia in 1917 and his descriptions of Kerensky.

Maugham's *Ashenden Stories* and Eric Ambler's *Coffin for Dimitrios*, for their brilliant descriptions of the technique of espionage; J. G. Farrell's extraordinary evocations of the Victorian state of mind, *The Siege of Krishnapur*, and of the Irish state of being, *Troubles;* Kipling's *Kim;* Joseph Conrad's *Under Western Eyes* and *The Secret Agent; One Hundred Years of Solitude* by Gabriel García Márquez; the eleventh edition of *The Encyclopedia Brittanica; The Oxford History of Technology*, as a guide to the connections between technical innovation and political movement; *Bartlett's Familiar Quotations*.

And, above all, *War and Peace*, that long meditation on the force of delusion in human affairs.

MARGE PIERCY

The poetry of William Blake, of William Wordsworth, of the Bible (particularly the Psalms and the Song of Solomon), Emily Dickinson, Walt Whitman, T. S. Eliot, William Carlos Williams, Edith Sitwell, Thomas Wyatt, Apollinaire, H.D., the poetry of D. H. Lawrence, of Yeats, of Keats — these are probably the most important of the early influences on my poetry. Elizabethan songs and folk songs also provided me with notions of sweet clarity.

Of modern poets, I have spent a lot of time reading Bertholt Brecht, Neruda, the early Auden, Rilke, Robert Duncan, Adrienne Rich, Audre Lorde, Vallejo, Maxine Kumin, Muriel Rukeyser, Margaret Atwood, Allen Ginsberg, Phillip and Nellie Sachs — these spring readily to mind. All such lists are extremely arbitrary and only reflect what comes to my mind at this moment. On another day the list would look different.

Of the novelists who have meant a lot to me, I would list Charles Dickens, Tolstoy, the Brontë sisters, Herman Melville, George Eliot, John Dos Passos, Gabriel García Márquez, Gertrude Stein and James Joyce. I probably have read Joyce's *Ulysses* and *Alice in Wonderland* and *Through the Looking Glass* more times than any other books.

Among contemporary novelists I immensely enjoy Margaret Atwood, Toni Morrison, Samuel Delaney, Joanna Russ, Thomas Keneally, Iris Murdoch, Stanislaw Lem and Manuel Puig.

My original notions of narrative arose from the Bible, from my grandmother's and my mother's storytelling, and from fairy tales and myths.

I enjoy good biographies, such as Richard Holmes's *Shelley: The Pursuit*, and autobiographies, such as

Vera Buch Weisbord's *Radical Life*. I like books that help me understand what's happening in the society, such as Robert Caro's *Power Broker: Robert Moses and the Fall of New York*, Robert Dumhoff's *Who Rules America Now* and Lillian Faderman's *Surpassing the Love of Men*, her groundbreaking study of female friendship.

Being very involved in Judaism, I enjoy reading works that help me, such as Gershom Scholem's *Kabbalah* or *Written Out of History* by Sandra Henry and Emily Taitz.

I enjoy natural history writers such as John Hay and Robert Finch.

There are certain books that all through my life have had a strong effect on me that don't fall into any of these categories. One is Jane Harrison's *Prolegomena to the Study of Greek Religion*. Others are *The Golden Bough* by James Frazer; Robert Graves's *White Goddess*; Susan Griffin's *Woman and Nature*; and *The Mermaid and the Minotaur* by Dorothy Dinnerstein.

Of course I should mention *The Second Sex* by Simone de Beauvoir, which stood alone for many years, in my mind and on my bookshelf, without companions concerned with the same topics.

Of all the Marxists I read, I think that Gorz and

Gramschi have meant the most to me. Sartre's *Being and Nothingness* and de Beauvoir's *Ethics of Ambiguity* were extremely important to me when I was in my early twenties.

Over the years I have loaned my books much too freely and I no longer have a copy of Elizabeth Fisher's erudite compilation of biology and anthropology and archaeology, so I cannot even produce the title accurately. Nonetheless, it was an important book to me.

Contributors

ISABEL ALLENDE, the exiled niece of Chile's assassinated president Salvador Allende, emerged as a major new voice in fiction in 1982 with her first novel, *The House of the Spirits*, which became a best seller both in Europe and in the United States. Her two subsequent novels are *Of Love and Shadows* and *Eva Luna*.

CHARLES McCARRY has written six novels about an American family named Christopher whose members have been involved in politics and secret intelligence from 1700 to the present: *The Last Supper*, *The Better Angels*, *The Secret Lovers*, *Tears of*

Autumn, *The Miernik Dossier*, and *The Bride of the Wilderness*.

MARGE PIERCY is a poet, a novelist, and a feminist. She is the author of ten novels — notably *Woman on the Edge of Time*, *Vida*, and *Gone to Soldiers* — and many volumes of poetry, most recently *Available Light*, in which the political issues of everyday life form a recurring theme.

ROBERT STONE is the author of four novels, which have as their animating current a concern for what's happening to America: *A Hall of Mirrors*, *Dog Soldiers*, which won the National Book Award for 1974, *A Flag for Sunrise*, and *Children of Light*. He has also taught at Harvard, Princeton, and other universities.

GORE VIDAL is a prolific author of novels, critical essays, and plays, including five hugely successful novels of American political history: *Burr*, *Lincoln*, *1876*, *Empire*, and *Washington, D.C.* The grandson of Senator Thomas Gore, he had twice run for political office himself, once in California and once in New York.

WILLIAM ZINSSER, a writer, editor, and teacher, is the author of thirteen books, including *On Writing Well*, *Writing to Learn*, and most recently *Spring Training*. He has been a newspaperman with the *New York Herald Tribune*, a columnist for *Life*, master of Branford College at Yale, and general editor of the Book-of-the-Month Club.